SPARK

9 Simple Strategies to Ignite
Exceptional Self-Leadership

Copyright © Sally Foley-Lewis 2021

All models copyright © Sally Foley-Lewis

ISBN 978-0-9874186-7-8

All rights reserved. No part of this publication may be reproduced or transmitted in any form or by any means, electronic or mechanical, including photocopying, recording, scanning or information storage and retrieval system without the prior written consent of the publisher.

The companion workbook is for personal use only. It cannot be copied, distributed or re-sold in part or full.

Every effort has been made to trace (and seek permission for use of) the primary source of material used in this book. Where the attempt has been unsuccessful, the publisher would be pleased to hear from the author/publisher to rectify any comission.

Cover Design: Lauren Forcey, Full Stop Writing, Editing and Design
Editing: Kristen Lowrey
Typesetting: @inkceptstudio

SPARK

9 Simple Strategies to Ignite Exceptional Self-Leadership

SALLY FOLEY-LEWIS

PRAISE FOR SPARK

Sally has pulled together nine strategies that any leader would be wise to adopt for greater success. Her addition of templates and guides makes this an interactive approach laser-focused on improving one's self.

—David Pace, Ph.D., Nuclear Energy Industry Research, Deputy Director

If you want to lead a team, or an organisation, you need to lead yourself first. Sally makes a compelling case to increase performance, productivity and ultimately profit, you need to start with self-leadership. This book contains 9 simple, powerful strategies for any leader willing to do the work on themselves to get the best out of everyone.

—Peter Cook, Author, The New Rules of Management

Self-leadership – it's such an integral component of every successful leader's journey. This wonderful book provides the how-to for any leader who is seeking great outcomes. You will enjoy this book, and the important messages it contains.

—Assistant Commissioner Andrew Short AFSM, Queensland Fire and Emergency Services

This book is essential reading for leaders, be they aspiring, new to leadership or experienced. It will appeal to anyone looking for ways to invigorate their leadership and build strong new behaviours. Sally is able to provide many insights into how we can develop our self-leadership, combining practical exercises and reflection activities with observations from her own leadership journey, and enhanced through compelling insights from a diverse range of leaders in her Spark interview series. This book has fired me up (again) and immediately joined my Go To library (once I have finished my homework)!

—Rowena Samaraweera, Customer Experience Design Lead, Insurance Industry

Sally's pragmatic approach once again shines through in her latest book, SPARK. The strategies in SPARK will ignite your confidence, influence and courage as you spark your self-leadership.

—Josh Grocke, Head of Client Engagement, Flight Centre Business Travel

That Sally Foley-Lewis would write a book entitled 'Spark' comes as absolutely no surprise. It's one of the most congruent titles imaginable, coming from an author who is so adept at helping others access the spark that lights them up. Leafing through the pages of this book, I'm seeing wisdom and courage in equal measure, carefully laid out such that the reader is invited to step up and find the spark that makes their leadership shine.

—Col Fink, Speaker and Adviser, Author of Speakership and Tribe of Learning.

Self-leadership – this is the how-to for any leader who wants more success. This is for any leader who wants more confidence, influence and courage in their career.

—**Mark Middleton, Group CEO, Icon Group**

SPARK is a must-read for any leader who wants more – more success driven by more confidence, more influence and more courage.

—**Dominique Lamb, CEO, National Retail Association**

If you are looking for one great idea, concept or a spark of genius as a leader, you will find it here. After reading Sally's book "SPARK", I found mine. Sally takes what can be complicated and make it simple and practical in today's world. This book is exactly what leaders are looking for and need. It is a five high and a thumbs up from me.

—**Jennifer Leone, Storytelling strategist in Business, Talk Trainers**

Self-leadership is rarely on a leader's to-do list, yet it is simply essential if you want to have better leaders leading organisations. In this book Sally Foley-Lewis lights the "Spark" for those aspiring to greater leadership and guides them through her nine carefully crafted and yet simple to apply strategies. It's an easy read with links to great video interviews with real self-leaders interspersed among the manuscript to keep you thinking and challenging the status quo. I think this will become an excellent go to text for those wanting to move up the leadership ladder and for those who have lost their "Spark" and need a refresher about where to next.

—**Lindsay Adams OAM, The Relationships Guy, CEO, 24x7 Assessments**

This book is the instruction manual for any leader who wants more self-leadership, success and is a must read for any leader who wants more confidence, influence and courage in their career.

—**Jeremy Fleming, CEO, Stagekings**

Sally has pulled together nine metacognitive strategies to embed across your professional development. Well worth adding to your reading list.

—**Sally Graham, National Manager, Learning & Teaching, Governance Institute of Australia Ltd**

Sally is one of those incredible women who when you meet her, you immediately feel her energy and her enthusiasm for everything she stands for. She actually is one person who truly walks her talk, and wants to see change in her area of expertise. As leaders we all should be striving daily to be the best we can be, to lead our teams together to great successful outcomes. This builds trust, loyalty, and creates a sense of pride and that wanting to be the best at what I do attitude. Sally helps you understand how simple it is to be that leader, who is long talked about for the right reasons even after you no longer lead that team. Sally congratulations on another incredible book that is going to see a whole new generation of leadership done the right way.

—**Tracey Mathers, CEO, Tracey Mathers Pty Ltd**

Sally's pragmatic approach once again shines through in her latest book, SPARK. The nine strategies she shares will help fire up your confidence, influence and courage as you spark your self-leadership.

—**Lisa Lockland-Bell, Vocal Coach, Performance Studios**

This book should contain the following warning - 'You will want to read this book slowly and at least three times'.

Spark is packed with thought provoking nuggets and practical exercises that help arm and inspire you to create a new you. Highly recommended if you have the ambition but need a nudge.

—Maz Farrelly, Creative Thinker & Keynote Speaker

I love this book! Sally has brought together 9 strategies that everyone can put into practice to develop that most important muscle of all: self-leadership.

Spark is inspiring reading for everyone because it's about the grit and honesty of what self-leadership is about, and as Sally explains is about that all-important relationship – the one you have with yourself!

There is an honesty, rawness and warmth in the accounts of those Sally has interviewed that makes this book extremely relatable. And the opportunities to record reflections only makes it feel even more like a personal journey into self-leadership. I'd like to see this book part of final year school or first year university so that our next generation starting out can gain the benefit of the wisdom and insights on an important topic. Investing in self-leadership benefits not just the individual, but also everyone with whom we come in contact including personal and professional relationships. This is a book that you won't just buy one – you'll buy multiple copies for friends and family to spread the Spark!

**—Professor (Law) Dr Caroline Hart,
Associate Head of School (Engagement),
University of Southern Queensland**

Sally's book SPARK is a quick and easy read, yet the ideas it contains are powerful. SPARK will quickly become a popular and influential book on leadership, its focus is on self-leadership and the strategies are clear in that before leading others you have to know how to lead yourself effectively, so you can apply what you learn to your personal and work life. When applied throughout an organisation, the guiding principles of self-leadership can result in a positive, transformative change in you and your workplace culture.

—Jo Sainsbury, Kickass Women, Advocate and Speaker, and Coal Train Driver

Sally has nailed it in her new book "Spark". Great insights on leadership and how to lean into your own style of leadership. Valid and useful ideas that provide a "spark" for leaders at every level!

—Rowdy McLean, Speaker, Author, Mentor, 2019 Keynote Speaker of the Year

For young Sally to spark her value, voice and
visibility in her first job,

and

every manager who wants to be a successful leader.

ABOUT THE AUTHOR

Sally Foley-Lewis is a self-leadership and middle management expert who has combined her skills from more than 20 years of leadership experience, including being a CEO, to dedicate her career to helping professionals achieve their goals and master their leadership skills.

Since 2010, Sally has directed her own company, focussing on helping managers lead through workshops, presentations and coaching. An author of multiple books, Sally works with clients from a wide range of industries, including from the banking, finance and legal sectors, government departments, corporate companies and community groups.

Having worked in the Middle East, including as a trade consultant for Austrade, and in Germany, Asia and across Australia, Sally has also been a CEO of a major youth program. She is a sought-after keynote speaker and leadership facilitator, as well.

In 2020 she was named the Breakthrough Speaker of the Year by Professional Speakers Australia and came away with a Gold and Bronze Award at the 'Stevie's' Women in Business 2020 Awards. In 2021 she was named University of Southern Queensland Outstanding Alumnus of the Year for Business and Enterprise.

She has also completed a Stand-Up Comedy Course, just to stay on her toes!

CONTENTS

About the Author		13
Acknowledgements		17
Introduction		19
Chapter 1	What is Self-Leadership?	25
Chapter 2	The Challenges	45
Chapter 3	The 3 'V's of Self-Leadership	53
Chapter 4	Value: It Starts Here!	61
Chapter 5	Self-Awareness: Know Thyself—Know Thy Value!	73
Chapter 6	Boundaries: Good Fences Make Good Neighbours	91
Chapter 7	Stand Up: Stand Up for Yourself, Even If No One is On Your Side.	101
Chapter 8	Voice: the Right Message, In the Right Tone, at the Right Time!	113
Chapter 9	Self-Talk: It's No One Else's Job to Like You!	123
Chapter 10	Interpersonal Communication Skills: The Real Connector for Personal and Professional Success!	133
Chapter 11	Speak Up: Who Does Your Silence Serve?	149
Chapter 12	Visibility: Being Seen at the Right Time for the Right Reason!	159
Chapter 13	Self-Image: You Determine Your Worth!	165
Chapter 14	Seen: An Ear, A Heart and An Insight to Help You Think and Self-Lead!	173

Chapter 15   Stand Out: Back Yourself to Get Out Front!................ 187
Chapter 16   Extra Self-Leadership Sparking Goals 199
Final Word.. 207
Book Sally 209
Sally's Other Books and Resources 213

ACKNOWLEDGEMENTS

I'm so grateful for the support I have in my life and career. It's an honour and a privilege to do the work I get to do and there are so many people who have contributed to making this work happen.

First and foremost, to my husband Martin who is one of the smartest, most grounded and calm people I have ever had the fortune to know. And he's mine! I appreciate his ongoing support and without it I would not be able to spend every day living my purpose to serve and help managers.

Throughout my career I have had amazing mentors who have guided, challenged and championed me in all areas of personal, professional and business development. I'm so grateful to them all: Jane Anderson, Peter Cook, Lindsay Adams, Lyndal Hansen and Jennifer Leonie. Just knowing you is a treasure but to have the benefit of your wisdom is life transforming.

When setting out to write this book I wanted to explore what other leaders thought of the concept of self-leadership. I reached out to leaders across a diverse range of industries: travel, nuclear energy, health, finance, education, insurance, retail, construction, technology, to name a few. I specifically sought out senior leaders as I suspected their experience would afford an insight and perspective on self-leadership worthy of discussion and sharing. What started as simple interviews for this book quickly transformed into a video series, I'm so grateful to the first cohort of senior leaders who willingly gave their time and insights: Dr Karina Butera, Andrew Short, Dr David Pace, Dr Caroline Hart, Sally Graham, Mark Middleton, Dominique Lamb,

Michelle Berriman, Sarah Markey-Hamm, Julie Garland-McLellan, Jo Sainsbury, Jeremy Fleming, Josh Grocke, Alison Flemming, Emma Barrie, Karen Brown, Lisa Lockland-Bell, Peter Williams, Rowena Samaraweera, DK Bakshi, Victor Perton and Jas Johal.

To my clients, you have inspired this book and inspired me to share the lessons that have served me and thousands of managers so well in the journey of leadership and self-leadership. Keep showing up and being the best version of yourself so others benefit from your greatness.

And to you, thank you for picking up this book and investing time and effort in continuing your journey to spark your best self.

INTRODUCTION

My first job right after graduating university was in 1992. It included the administrative task of ordering supplies and resources for the whole team. This was in a time long before online ordering and internal intranets that streamlined such processes. Instead, I had a carbonless copy order book, and a physical catalogue folder of printed pages all stored in plastic sleeves.

To order anything, from major operational supplies to a litre of milk, I had to sign the order and send the page off in an interoffice envelope. It was all very official and my signature was required on any order for it to be fulfilled.

After returning from some annual leave, I came to do some ordering and as I was turning pages to find the next available page, I noticed the last page that had an order had my signature but it was not me who signed it. The order was made while I was away. As I looked at the signature it hit me.

I felt heat rise in my stomach, then in my chest, and then in my throat. I looked up and blurted out, 'My signature has been forged.'

I was not really addressing anyone in particular, and I hadn't really taken in who else was in the office when I said it. It was really an emotive reaction that I just blurted out without thinking. But my boss happened to be nearby and, with a flippant indignation replied, 'It was only for a litre of milk.' This instantly gave away that she was the person who forged my signature.

The casual way she said that hit me like a massive punch to the face. I was completely taken aback. In that moment, it felt like my voice was taken away from me. I felt tiny and powerless. And I felt that I couldn't challenge her actions.

The rest of that day was a fog. I questioned myself as to whether this was a big deal or not. Do I write it off because it was simply for milk? Or is this a big deal because someone forged my signature? My boss' tone threw me for a massive curve ball.

All that night I churned through unpleasant emotions. I was angry. I was furious. I was fuming. I was angry at myself because I knew it wasn't about the milk really. I was furious that someone I trusted had done something so against the values I thought we shared. I was fuming that I didn't say anything to let her know what she did was not okay. Instead, I let that situation go. I didn't stand up for myself and I didn't speak up.

You can imagine that this was the end of feeling comfortable, safe and open around my boss. The remainder of my days with that team were often filled with anxiety. I wondered, if my boss was prepared to forge my signature what else might she do?

Back then psychological safety wasn't a term spoken about. However, this was a clear example of someone not feeling psychologically safe. I didn't feel as though I could speak up without the risk of backlash. Our relationship was never the same. I left as quickly as I could find another job.

This incident—when I was just starting my career—rocked me to my core. It was a defining moment for my own personal growth and self-leadership. The anger I felt following that incident spurred in me a desire to first and foremost strive to work in an environment that's safe and where values are aligned. Of course, we don't all have to have the same values all the time. That's unrealistic. But there needs to be some alignment so that we all feel comfortable and safe working with each other.

Since that first job, almost 30 years ago, I have worked hard to find my balance with speaking out and standing up for myself. In those early years I may not have done it well sometimes. I may have been too quiet at times, and too loud at other times. That's the learning process.

I have invested in my self-leadership through increasing my self-awareness and pushing myself to do those things that expand my perspective and world view—that challenge my assumptions and strengthen my integrity. I have invested in myself, expanding my emotional intelligence, so that I have the confidence to speak up and stand up for myself, and others. I am able to identify and regulate my emotions so that I can manage myself and respond appropriately to most situations I'm thrown into. I'm actually quite well known for being able to read a room well.

In the beginning I didn't know the work was self-leadership, but I can clearly see that was exactly what it was, and it continues now.

This deliberate self-leadership work has helped to land me in some amazing places and roles. I've lived and worked in Europe and the Middle East, as well as outback Australia. I've held diverse leadership roles, including being the CEO of a youth program. And today I work with managers all over the world to build their leadership capability.

I've been fortunate to travel the world delivering keynote speeches, workshops, coaching and in-depth leadership programs to help transform people. In this work, time and again, self-leadership has been an essential ingredient that sets the scene for exceptional leadership.

Self-leadership is a journey. It's not set and forget. It is the ongoing effort to lead oneself. And it's a vital part of building your success as a leader of others.

This book will give you nine strategies for igniting your self-leadership. These are by no means the only strategies but they are aligned with three core areas of focus—value, voice and visibility—that will give you structure for amplifying your self-leadership.

In this book we'll take time with each focus area. Each one offers you the opportunity to explore the inner workings of who you are, your self-awareness, self-talk and self-image. All of which impacts how you interact with the world around you, how you connect and influence others, how you lead and how you are led. You will learn how the boundaries you set and your interpersonal communication skills influence your self-leadership as well as demonstrate the strength of your self-leadership. You'll also discover how mentors and networking are critical for helping you grow and be visible.

The strategies in this book are tested, practical and implementable. Some can have an immediate impact on your confidence while others may take some time to dive into. But all the strategies are doable and are presented here in a logical sequence that will help you implement them easily into your own life. And, of course, if you need help with any along the way, please reach out. I'd be delighted to help.

In the process of creating this book I reached out to executives and senior leaders across a range of industries and countries to explore their perspective on self-leadership. The first cohort of interviews have become a video series you can access at https://www.sallyfoleylewis.com/spark/. I've added relevant quotes from these interviews among the pages of this book.

As you read through this book I want you to consider:

- When have you had your values challenged?
- When have you felt as though your voice was taken, quietened or stopped?
- When have you felt challenged or stopped in your tracks so that you couldn't stand up for yourself?

As you work through the nine strategies, you'll see your self-leadership (and then your leadership of others) ignite and grow.

This is a book full of practical strategies, you have space provided in this book to capture your insights, answers to questions, actions and reflections. Not everyone likes to write in books so you can use the companion workbook, an editable pdf, which you can access here: https://bit.ly/SPARKbookwkbk.

What did you wish you knew about self-leadership before you stepped into your first leadership role?

I wish I was bolder, earlier.

Mark Middleton
Global CEO, Icon Group

Snap to watch
the full interview.

Mark's unspoken message to 'go for it' shows that his experience can teach others that we could all do with being a bit bolder earlier on so as to seize opportunities sooner in our careers and lives. Not every bold act will yield a positive outcome but it will give lessons and experiences others, less bold, will not benefit from.

When my husband and I moved from Australia to the United Arab Emirates I had already had an expat experience but it was new for him. In our planning, he asked me, 'What happens when we go?' My response was, 'We miss our family, friends, a wedding or two, funerals, births; but we'll make new friends, learn a new culture, experience a culture deeper than being a tourist, travel. And if we don't like it, we come home.' Martin replied, 'Well, don't sugar coat it!'

Spark your self-leadership by saying yes even when it feels scary. Say yes even when you have that 'but I don't know if it'll work' moment. Be bold!

CHAPTER ONE
WHAT IS SELF-LEADERSHIP?

Influencing Oneself

Many definitions of leadership include the element of influence; such as, *leadership is influencing others to perform*. From that definition it follows that just as leadership is influencing others, *self-leadership* is *influencing oneself*.

Research[1] shows that the idea of self-leadership has developed primarily from social cognitive theory and intrinsic motivation theory, though it is also influenced by multiple other theories. In fact, the following theories have all influenced the development of the concept and process of self-leadership:

- Self-Regulation: the ability to guide your own thoughts, feelings and behaviours to reach your goals.
- Self-Management: your ability to deliberately—consciously—manage your thoughts, feelings and behaviours.
- Positive Psychology: the scientific study of positive aspects of life, focusing on individual and societal well-being.
- Self-Determination: the motivation behind the choices you make without external influences or interferences.

---

1 Neck, Manz, Houghton. 2017. Self-Leadership: The definitive guide to personal excellence.

- Goal Setting: the ability to put specific goals into clear plans to achieve a desired outcome.

With all those theories in play, it might be difficult to nail down what self-leadership is exactly. But the definition is actually quite simple.

'Self-leadership strategies are designed to result in intentional activities that can help people reshape their behaviour and cognitive processes to be more positive and productive.'[2]

In other words, self-leadership takes into account what you do, why you do what you do and how you should do that.

A Lifelong Journey

Self-leadership is a lifelong journey of learning and influencing oneself. It cannot be a set and forget. As you learn and grow from one experience, another experience will come along and help, or challenge, you to further grow and develop.

This aligns well with Dr Carol Dweck's seminal work on mindset. As Dweck asks in her book *Mindset: The New Psychology of Success*[3], 'is success about learning or proving you're smart?'. Work, life, family, friends, colleagues, bosses, direct reports, and of course, crises such as pandemics, work from home mandates, and the fallout from crises such as the projected great resignation from the COVID-19 pandemic, will throw more than enough challenges your way. And as Dweck's research shows, a fixed mindset would be totally focusing on succeeding. On the other hand, a growth mindset is about stretching oneself and becoming smarter. A growth mindset seeks to find a way to adapt and overcome.

---

[2] Neck, Manz, Houghton. 2017. Self-Leadership: The definitive guide to personal excellence.
[3] Dweck, Carol S. Mindset: The New Psychology of Success. New York: Random House, 2006.

Your journey of self-leadership involves consistently stretching yourself. To self-lead, it takes motivation or drive. It takes curiosity and, probably most importantly, an active and deliberate decision to be a self-leader. Ultimately, it is a journey. And in the infinitely wise words of Dr Suess[4].

> 'You have brains in your head.
> Your feet in your shoes.
> You can steer yourself in any direction you choose.'

Although it's a children's book, I gift Dr Suess' book, *Oh, The Places You'll Go!*, to many managers I work with. Their responses to me when receiving and reading the book are moving and endearing. Here's a few:

> *'I simply loved this book when I was a child but it really does make sense to me today. Thank you for helping me realise my choices and potential.'*
>
> *'I gave a copy of this to my children but I really should have been reading it for myself too. The message is so powerful.'*
>
> *'Thank you. I cried when I read this because it reminded me I had forgotten that I have everything I need to find my way, including the ability to ask for help.'*

---

4 Seuss, Dr. Oh, the Places You'll Go! New York: Random House, 1990.

'Would you want to follow you?'
—Sally Foley-Lewis

What did you wish you knew about self-leadership before you stepped into your first leadership role?

I wish I knew it was a tool I had all along!
And learning when to let go of the reliance on others and build your own self-reliance.

Alison Flemming
General Manager, Scentre Group

Snap to watch
the full interview.

What a great message from Alison. It's time to recognise you have self-leadership and self-reliance already within you.

Spark your self-leadership by letting it be more present in your day to day.

Why Self-Leadership Matters

Have you ever made a mistake when cooking? It doesn't take much to imagine what happens when salt is used instead of sugar. The end result may closely look like the recipe photo, but once you taste it you realise that the similarity ends there. And the recipe has really not gone to plan.

1. **Every ingredient has a purpose: but you're the most important ingredient!**

In their research into self-leadership, Prussia, Anderson and Manz, found that self-leadership strategies had a significant effect on self-efficacy evaluations, and that self-efficacy directly affects performance[5]. Self-efficacy is the belief that you can succeed at tasks—that you've got the capacity to handle what is expected or given to you.

When it comes to the success of your business, organisation, team and even your leadership, the ingredients of success are a combination of strategy, operations, people and, most importantly, you. What *you* do, how *you* show up, how *you* interact, how *you* lead yourself and others impacts your performance, the team culture and efficacy, and, of course, the bottom line.

There will always be many things out of your control. But not when it comes to the essential ingredient of *you*. You can control you. You can influence yourself. And you do have the power to build and maintain your self-leadership.

2. **Self-Leadership also impacts team performance**

Effective self-leadership makes for effective team members, who positively and productively contribute towards the ultimate success of the team. Successful leaders not only focus on their own self-leadership, but they also spark the self-leadership in their direct

---

[5] Neck, Manz, Houghton. 'Self-Leadership: The Definitive Guide to Personal Excellence', 2016. Sage Publications.

reports. They create the space for effective, empowered individual contributors to the team.

When each individual has strong self-leadership, they are responsible, accountable and doing their part. Self-leadership teams have the respect, courage and permission to challenge assumptions; empower each other; go the extra mile without over-stepping boundaries; drive performance from a shared goal or vision; and celebrate individual and group successes.

3. Self-leadership creates successful organisations

When it comes to the success of your organisation, you, and more specifically your leadership, has the power to influence. Strong leadership comes from exceptional self-leadership because self-leadership comes from a strong sense of self-awareness, confidence, emotional intelligence, drive and efficacy. This means you'll have the confidence and courage to contribute, and be a powerful and positive influence to support, guide and lead your team members, to stand out among your peers and to help realise the strategic vision of the business.

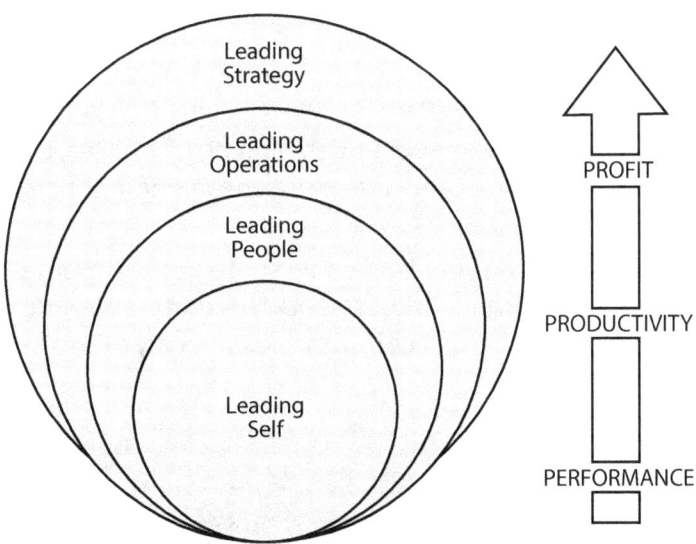

The founder of modern management and inventor of the concepts of management by objectives and self-control, Peter Drucker, advises that success as a leader comes to those who know themselves—'their strengths, their values, and how they best perform'[6]. And Daniel Goleman, author of the world-renowned book, *Emotional Intelligence*, explains that exceptional leaders distinguish themselves because of superior self-leadership[7].

Study after study consistently link self-leadership and positive individual outcomes via creativity, innovation, resilience, efficacy, job satisfaction and job performance. These researchers and thought leaders, and many others, demonstrate the value of self-leadership. They show that when successful leaders work on their own self-leadership, they will help spark their team members' self-leadership as well.

The benefits of self-leadership

Actively engaging in strategies that expand, improve and enhance your self-leadership has many benefits.

1. The more you learn about yourself, the more curious you can become to learn more.
2. The more exposed you are to how you think about yourself in a different range of situations, the more this can open your mind.
3. The more you expand on your understanding of yourself, the more wise you can become and the more meaningful your life can become.
4. The more you expand your leadership strategies, the more excited you become for others' success and the more you strip away jealousy of others and replace it with inspiration by others' success.

---

6 Drucker, Peter F. Managing Oneself. Harvard Business Review Press, 2008.
7 Goleman, Daniel. Emotional Intelligence. New York: Bantam Books, 1995. Print.

5. The more you embrace yourself, the happier you can become, the more courage you'll have to try new and different things and the more confident you become to speak up, to stand out.
6. The more you elevate your self-leadership, the more you can contribute to your team, organisation, community and society and the more productive you can be.

> If you want to lead, invest at least 40% of your time in leading yourself.
> —Dee Hock, Founder of VISA

What did you wish you knew about self-leadership before you stepped into your first leadership role?

I wish I had had more self-belief, but then it is something you develop with time and experience.

Sally Graham
**National Manager,
Learning & Teaching at
Governance Institute of Australia**

Snap to watch
the full interview.

What experiences have you already had in your career or in your life that remind you that you have self-belief?

Spark your self-leadership by reflecting on how much you have achieved, lived through and experienced so far.

The Self-Leadership Ladder

In a world of busy, constant distractions and the pull of multiple priorities, focusing on self-leadership can be the last thing on an already full to-do list. A 'spark' can be helpful to remind you to focus on self-leadership.

Why a spark? A spark is something that sets off a sudden force. A spark is instant and short lived, but it can ignite something greater. And a spark can be the pattern or habit breaker for you to choose self-leadership.

A spark can fire up your focus on self-leadership. It can be the motivator and reminder that you matter and as such your self-leadership matters.

Reflect on the levels within this ladder and see where you may find yourself. Naturally you may be higher, having stronger self-leadership, some days while others are tougher, more challenging days and you might be a little lower on the ladder.

This ladder can give you an indication of what you can do to shift towards greater self-leadership and success in your leadership and career.

The Spark Activity Ladder

	ACTIVITY	FOCUS	SELF-LEADERSHIP
5	LEADING SELF	ACCEPT	SPARK
4	DEFINING SELF	APPLY	SIZZLE
3	SKILLING SELF	ACQUIRE	STARTER
2	DISCOVERING SELF	AWAKE	SPUTTER

Level One—Neglecting Self

At this lowest level, you are actively avoiding your self-leadership. You're neglecting your own development and so in many facets of your life and throughout the day-to-day you will feel stalled. You may find your energy is stalled and your confidence and influence, as well. At this level people tend to avoid or minimise the amount of interaction they have with you because they feel like they're dealing with someone who's emotionally clueless.

Neglect of yourself can happen in the short term when life's demands are overwhelming and there's too much going on. However continuing this habit over the long term will have significant negative effects on your career, your happiness and even your wellness.

To shift out of this level is to wake up to the neglect and its impact on yourself and others.

Level Two—Discovering Self

Having found a sense of awakening you can discover more about yourself. I like to think of this level as a self-realisation moment. For example, when I give keynote speeches about self-leadership, I invite the audience (and you can do this too, if you like) to stand up, ground their feet comfortably hip width apart and now relax the muscles in their bottoms. In that moment they generally think one of two things:

1. 'Those muscles weren't tensed'; or
2. 'Wow, how did she know that?'

The audience has a giggle and they realise they've discovered something—they've had a self-realisation moment. This is how I describe this level of the ladder—the beginning of discoveries.

Will everyone stand and release those muscles every single time from that point on? No. Waking up to the realisation and discovering more of yourself is like when an engine sputters.

To shift up to greater self-leadership, these discoveries about yourself need to ramp up and you must acquire more and more understanding, skills and knowledge.

Level Three—Skilling Self

At this level you're open in search self-realisation moments and you've begun to build on your skills and knowledge. I like to think of this stage as embracing the Red Car Syndrome.

The Red Car Syndrome is based on the Baader Meinhof Phenomenon[8]. It asserts that once you see, buy or learn something new, suddenly you see or are confronted with that thing everywhere. In the same way, once you are awake to the skills and knowledge you can acquire, you then see opportunities around you to reflect and learn about what you do, why you do what you do, and how you should do that or could something better.

---

8 Zwicky, Arnold M. 'Why are we so illuded?' Stanford University. 2006. Accessed at https://web.stanford.edu/~zwicky/LSA07illude.abst.pdf on 15 November 2021.

This level is the most aligned to shifting from conscious incompetence to conscious competence as noted in management trainer Martin Broadwell's, four levels of teaching[9]. You become very conscious of what you don't yet know and what you're learning[10].

To shift to the next level, you take this learning and apply it to your self-leadership, life and leadership of others.

Level Four—Defining Self

If you choose to constantly grow and evolve you get to define who you are. This level is about taking the learning you're constantly doing and using that to define who you are, who you choose to be and how you choose to behave. For example, it's quite well accepted that your values are set from your beliefs, background, education and networks. What you also can do is choose your values and choose to behave in accordance with values that will serve you well.

To shift to the highest level is to put the learning and defining into your everyday way of living.

Level Five—Leading Self

When you are leading yourself, you accept that learning and defining are ongoing. You experience sparks often that can set off a sudden opportunity to grow and become an even better version of yourself. And you make learning and growing a habit, a part of your everyday, so you consistently gain the benefits of self-leadership. You

---

9 Conger, D. Stuart; Mullen, D (December 1981). 'Life skills'. International Journal for the Advancement of Counselling. Accessed at https://doi.org/10.1007%2FBF00118327 on 17 November 2021.

10 The four levels of teaching, as described by management trainer Martin M. Broadwell, suggests that you will shift from 1. unconscious incompetence (you don't realise that you don't know or understand something), to 2. conscious incompetence (you realise you don't know or understand something), to 3. conscious competence (you know how to do something but it takes considerable concentration, or e.g. broken down into smaller steps, as this is new), to 4. unconscious competence (you have so much practice and ability with something that it becomes second nature).

become adept at exploring what you do, what drives you, why you do what you do and how you could something better.

It's important to note that, from a productivity perspective, it's not always about adding more and more, or doing more and more. It's about learning more and more about you and more and more ways of skilling yourself to help you do what you do better.

At the fifth level, accepting the ongoing development of self-awareness, self-knowledge and self-confidence means igniting or sparking success can be found consistently. Sparking your self-leadership is not about winning and succeeding all the time. As great as that would be, it's not realistic. It's also not about never making mistakes, nor experiencing failure, or falling short of others' expectations. Instead, it's about how you handle these situations that make for a positive and successful difference. It's knowing how to bounce back, to step up again, to learn from the mistakes and do better next time. It's understanding that success and self-leadership are naturally intertwined.

In a world of information overload, there can be so much that distracts and attracts. Many leaders are at capacity so it's important to be discerning. There are many more strategies that can be implemented. But the nine strategies in this book have been chosen to be doable for self-leadership and designed to fit into the busy lifestyle of leaders and not to overwhelm with too much 'to do' work.

Success and self-leadership are naturally intertwined.
—Sally Foley-Lewis

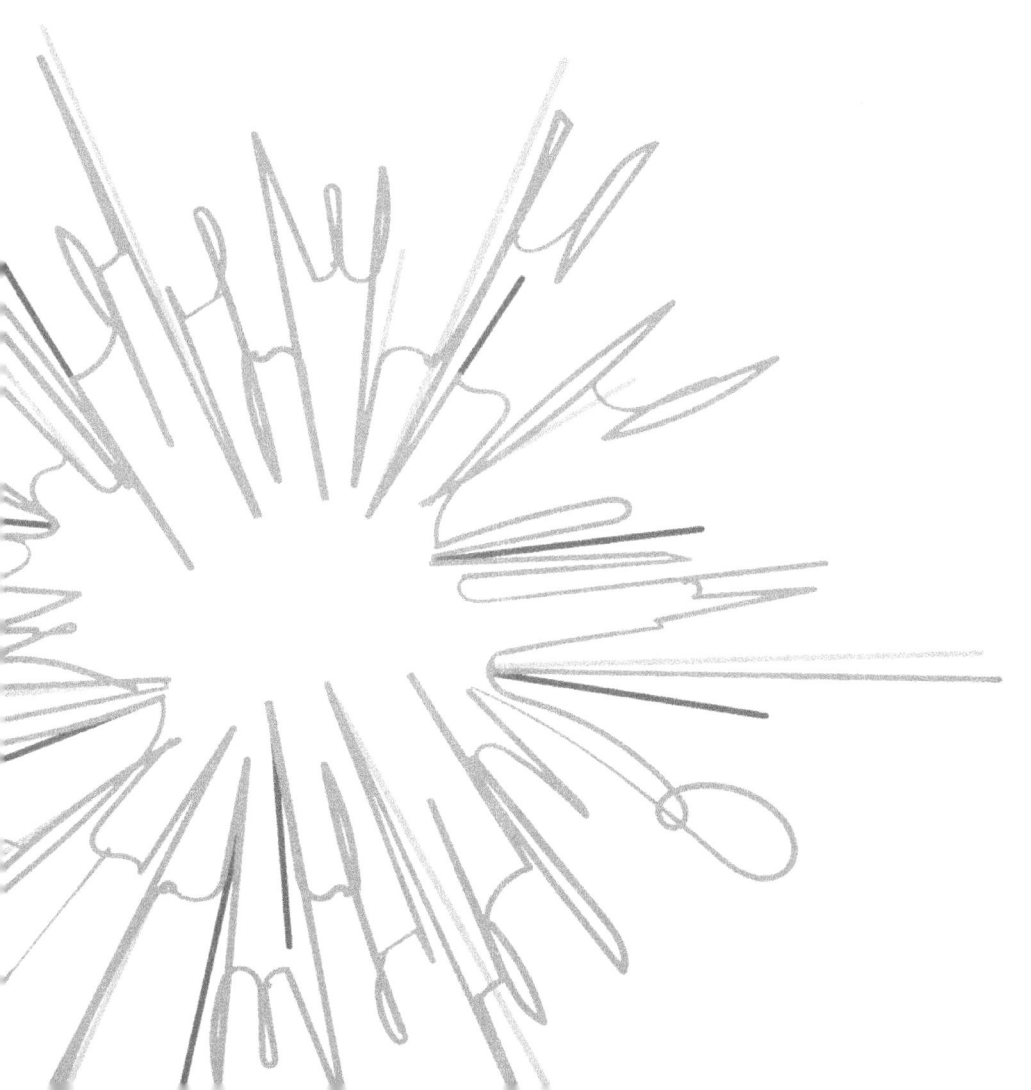

Practice: Your Self-Leadership Insights

Reflect on the last stressful day you had. Looking at the SPARK Activity Ladder, at what level would you say you were operating?

_____
_____
_____

What comes to mind when you think of yourself at that level?

_____
_____
_____

Reflect on the last really productive and successful day you had. At what level you would you say you were operating?

_____
_____
_____

What comes to mind when you think of yourself at that level?

_____
_____
_____

Where do you see yourself on the SPARK Activity Ladder?

_____
_____
_____

Why do you want to spark your self-leadership?

_____
_____
_____

If you had exceptional self-leadership, what do you think your life would be like?

_____
_____
_____

Who do you see or know who has exceptional self-leadership?

_____
_____
_____

What makes them, in your opinion, have exceptional self-leadership?

_____
_____
_____

What did you wish you knew about self-leadership before you stepped into your first leadership role?

I'm the only one who sees things the way I see it.

Andrew Short ASFM
*Assistant Commissioner,
Qld Fire and Emergency Services*

Snap to watch the full interview.

What I like about this quote from Andrew is that it reminds you that your opinion, your view on something, is just that—one person's view. Others will not see the same situation, problem or opportunity in exactly the same way you do.

Spark your self-leadership by remembering that the world is full of diverse perspectives and views that help us grow, learn and add to our wisdom.

CHAPTER TWO
THE CHALLENGES

When Self-Leadership is Needed

Over the years I have worked with thousands of managers and leaders in their leadership development, and the most common thing that is evident is that most want to do well. Most want to be good leaders doing good work. Most are keen to be productive and positive contributors to the team, the work, their own leadership and the organisation.

Despite the desire and drive to do well there are common challenges managers and leaders share with me. A lack of self-awareness and self-leadership, potentially having a lack lustre inner drive and struggling with speaking up, can create challenges to productivity, performance, culture and career success. For example:

Communication

> 'I struggle to have the difficult conversations. I don't want to be the 'bad guy' or get accused of bullying. I just end up avoiding it all.'

Not having a clear sense of what you need to say, the outcome you want and how to communicate to be understood will lead to increased stress, dancing around the issue or simply avoiding the critical conversations.

Personal Productivity

> *'I come in super early so I can have some time to myself to get my work done.'*
>
> *'Because of the pandemic and work from home, I get a lot of work done. I seem to work even longer hours but I don't see my team much and that leaves me worried about how productive they are being.'*

Self-leadership involves understanding your value and drivers which are linked to boundaries. Identifying, setting and holding healthy boundaries helps boost productivity. John Pencavel, an economics professor from Stanford University found that productivity per hour declined sharply when people worked more than 50 hours a week[11]. He found that beyond 55 hours of work is pointless as you won't be any more productive.

Delegating and Trust

> *'Everyone seems to already be too busy so I can't delegate anything to anyone.'*
>
> *'It's just quicker if I do it myself.'*
>
> *'I don't trust that they'll do the work to the standard I want.'*

Leaders with exceptional self-leadership will have the self-awareness and emotional intelligence needed to communicate expectations, to help their people prioritise so they may be available for delegation opportunities and build stronger trusting relationships with the team. Weak relationships will have weak trust. Strong relationships will have strong trust.

---

[11] Pencavel, John. 2015. 'The Productivity of Working Hours,' Economic Journal, Royal Economic Society, vol. 125(589), pages 2052-2076, December.

Control and Micromanaging

> *'I can't see my team so how do I know if they're getting their work done?'*

Micromanagement is one of the quickest ways to turn off creativity, passion and productivity in a team. It's one of the biggest reasons that employees leave an organisation. And when a leader controls others through micromanaging, they're just covering up their own leadership flaws.

On the other hand, a leader with strong self-leadership engages and empowers rather than dictates and micromanages. They act from within, sincerely and honestly. And with a mature, integrated self with high emotional intelligence they can act as a stable guide to others.

Decision Making

> *'I often feel as though critical information is being held back and that makes it hard to make decisions.'*
>
> *'If I make a decision and it goes wrong I'm worried about the backlash.'*
>
> *'I feel like the world is on my shoulders and I have to have all the answers.'*

Without self-leadership leaders may lack the confidence and self-assurance to be open to suggestions and ideas. This can lead to limited decision making, and therefore missed opportunities for creativity and innovation. Self-leaders have the courage to make decisions knowing they are doing the best they can with the information available and have the efficacy to adjust as things unfold.

Missed Opportunities

> *'I left that meeting kicking myself. I should've put forward the idea I had. Now I don't know how to get my voice heard.'*
>
> *'I'm sick of being overlooked. How do I get to be seen and get an opportunity to step up?'*

Self-leaders know that the only thing that overcomes missed opportunities is making opportunities happen. Waiting to be asked is expecting others to work out that you want an opportunity. It's expecting them to be mind readers. But mind reading just leads to confusion—and instead of saving time, or giving you the outcomes that you need, it could instead have the opposite consequences.

Guilt

> *'If I spend any time for myself I feel guilty but I also feel like I've lost myself in trying to be and do everything for everyone else.'*

Great leadership starts with self-leadership, and it's exactly like the safety message on an aeroplane—you are required to put your oxygen mask on yourself first before you can help others. In other words, it's about putting yourself in the best position to give your best. You can't give your best when you're running on empty. So, spending time on yourself is not something to feel guilty about, but something to embrace and honour. And it will make you a better leader in the end.

Imposter Syndrome

> *'I sometimes wonder if I'm actually cut out for this job.'*
>
> *'I am not sure if I can ask or put my hand up. What if they work out I'm not the right person for the job?'*

Leaders often wonder if they are really cut out for their role. They question if they are good enough to be an effective and productive leader. Imposter syndrome is very common, and it can be debilitating too. Working on your self-leadership will give you the confidence to identify your value and personal power.

There will no doubt be challenges you face from time-to-time or day-to-day. Ignoring those challenges can give some short-term relief but unless you deal with them, they will just keep appearing when you least expect them. Dealing with the challenges can equip you with the skills and experiences to handle similar challenges in the future.

Actively working on your self-leadership will give you the confidence, influence and courage to stand up for what you and your team needs. It will help you to speak up so that yours is a voice of calm and reason, letting you handle whatever is thrown your way. Of course things will still go wrong or you'll still have awkward situations, but you'll have everything you need in your toolkit to handle it all.

Practice: Your Self-Leadership Insights

What are the top three challenges in your role?

1. _____

2. _____

3. _____

How would it feel if these challenges were no longer a challenge for you?

_____
_____

What would you do if you had more confidence?

_____
_____

What would you do if you had more influence?

_____
_____

What would you do if you had more courage?

_____
_____

What did you wish you knew about self-leadership before you stepped into your first leadership role?

There is actually nothing wrong with failing. I think people only equate leadership with the sense of success. It's okay to fail.

Professor (Law) Dr Caroline Hart
Associate Head of School (Engagement),
University of Southern Queensland

Snap to watch
the full interview.

What I like about Caroline's perspective is that life is not about a constant and consistent stream of wins and successes. That simply isn't real life. Real life for you as a leader is a roller-coaster ride of wins, challenges and disappointments. The failures help build resilience, experience and wisdom. They might not feel great but they offer huge value. The learnings and the wins can reinforce your value and help boost your confidence.

Spark your self-leadership by remembering the last time something failed. What did it teach you about the situation and about yourself?

Self-leadership always precedes team leadership.
—Michael Hyatt

CHAPTER THREE
THE 3 'V'S OF SELF-LEADERSHIP

Spark your Value, Voice and Visibility

Self-leadership is rarely on a leader's to-do list. It can be a challenge to focus on when every day is consumed with getting work done and helping direct reports get their work done. Making self-leadership development simple is essential if you want to have better leaders leading organisations.

As you work through the nine strategies in this book you can decide to jump from one strategy to another in any order that resonates for you and as you see a need. However, there is a natural progression that starts with value, then works through voice and then visibility.

The SPARK Model

This is the core approach to sparking self-leadership. The three V's are value, voice and visible.

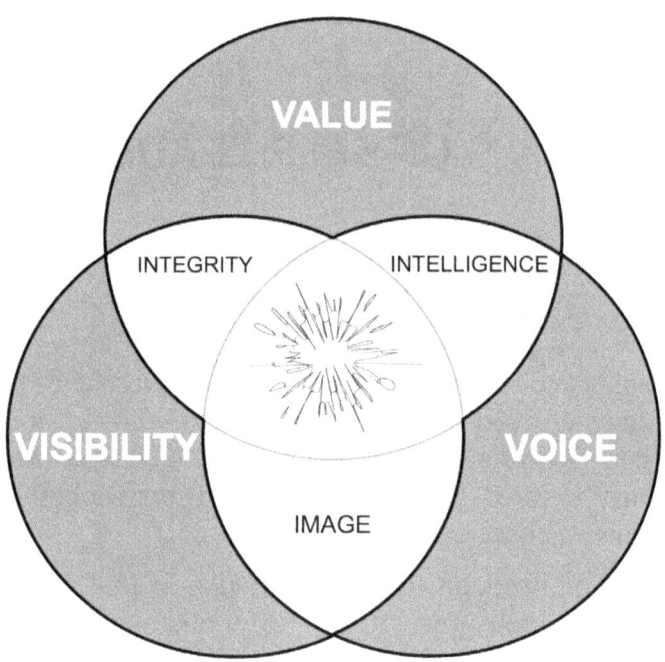

1. Value

Start with value because identifying your core values is foundational for how you behave and lead. The first three strategies are designed to help you understand and amplify your value. This starts with self-awareness.

Self-awareness is about knowing and understanding your own character and feelings, and is linked to emotional intelligence. Emotional intelligence is a massive topic in itself and if you would like more information on this, including undertaking an emotional intelligence assessment with a debrief session please do reach out to me.

An important part of value is setting boundaries, which, among other things, demonstrates your value to yourself. This first part will also explore what it means to stand up, identify your own value in an organisation and value your own contribution.

2. Voice

Your words or thoughts directed to yourself are your self-talk. Do you even know what you say to yourself?

In this portion of voice, you'll explore self-talk and how it can impact your self-leadership. The inner work of self-talk will then shift to the interpersonal and link your interpersonal communication skills to self-leadership and leading.

Knowing when to contribute and knowing that others are waiting on your voice is an important concept to grasp as you spark your self-leadership. Speaking up is often a conundrum for leaders. It can be especially difficult in meetings to know when to speak up or shut up. In this section we'll help you uncover strategies for speaking up.

3. Visibility

Think of being visible as a little like a makeover show without the wardrobe or make up. Anyone who's had a makeover will tell you that the impact is more than just an improvement or amplification in what they wear. It also boosts self-image and confidence.

I had a professional image consultant work with me and during the process she would dare me to try on clothes I would never have thought to try. I came out of the dressing room in tears after trying on one outfit because I realised how good the outfit looked and how great I felt. The clothes were the mechanism but the process was the key to helping boost my confidence and encourage me to stand out.

In the same way, focusing on your visibility will spark your self-leadership. The people you connect with, who you are visible to, can open your world to opportunities and experiences. As self-made millionaire and motivational speaker, Jim Rohn says, 'You are the average of the five people you spend the most time with', meaning your network is an essential part of developing you and sparking your self-leadership via your visibility.

Mentoring is also an essential part of your self-leadership journey. You'll explore strategies to spark your visibility in this part. If the inner work is self-image and how you see yourself, then showing up is the proof. You'll explore what showing up means for your success as a leader and self-leader.

The 3 'I's of Self-Leadership—Intelligence, Image, Integrity

As the SPARK Model shows, when your value and voice are aligned, you'll be seen as intelligent. Not just someone who's clever but someone with wisdom, emotional intelligence and social intelligence.

When your voice and visibility are aligned, you'll have a positive image across the team, the organisation and in the eyes of those who could positively influence your career.

And when your visibility and value are aligned, you'll be known for your integrity.

Self-Leadership Sparks Confidence, Influence and Courage

Without strong self-leadership, leaders will find any insecurities they may have will loom large and could impact on their ability to lead productively. Insecurity shows up in many ways such as micromanaging, indecision and avoiding delegation.

Complacency has been referred to as the silent killer of business—being self-satisfied while being unaware of any negative culture, deficiencies or dangers in effort or performance. The complacent leader will have a sense of being satisfied, which in and of itself is not bad, but as customers, competitors and opportunities constantly evolve it's the high performing leader who empowers their team to keep one step ahead. A leader with strong self-leadership will have the courage to keep pushing the organisation forward; they use their influence to keep the team performing, and have the courage to challenge any complacency.

When big challenges like a crisis hit, leaders can naturally be and feel confounded as they work to make sense of what's happening and what's to happen when so much is unknown. Strong self-leadership will help leaders shift through that feeling of being confounded quickly so they can make the decisions their people need, they can influence those around them to come on the journey through a crisis or change, and have the confidence of knowing that even with so much unknown they can work their way through the situation.

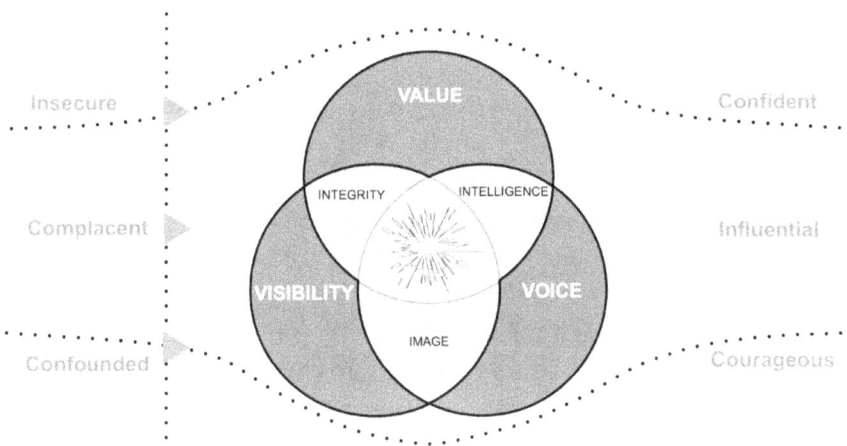

Sparking your self-leadership through the three areas of value, voice and visibility will help leaders move on from any sense of insecurity, complacency and confoundment.

Leaders need confidence so they can communicate both the good, and the challenging, messages to their team. Confidence gives leaders the capacity to stay calm amidst a crisis or to correct mistakes without losing face. Confidence helps decision making, so leaders can shift away from indecision or stagnation. Confident leaders will embrace the unknown and complex to help themselves, their team and their organisation thrive through change, uncertainty or crisis.

For leaders to implement change, drive performance or get their ideas over the line, they need to influence. They need to be seen as having influence. In Robert B. Cialdini's classic 2001 book, *Influence*, he shares, those 'who don't know how to get people to say yes soon fall away; those who do, stay and flourish', (page xii). You don't have to have a leadership title to have influence. But without influence a person is going to be a somewhat ineffective leader or have inconsistent results.

Courage is seen almost every day, in our emergency services workers who save lives, put out fires and choose to go toward the danger rather than retreat. Courage in leadership is, as Kathleen Reardon shares in a *Harvard Business Review* article, more of a special kind of calculated risk taking. She goes on to say that:

> 'people who become good leaders have a greater than average willingness to make bold moves, but they strengthen their chances of success—and avoid career suicide—through careful deliberation and preparation. Business courage is not so much a visionary leader's inborn characteristic as a skill acquired through decision-making processes that improve with practice. In other words, most great business leaders teach themselves to make high-risk decisions.'[12]

In times of uncertainty, change and crisis leadership takes courage! On any given day, but during ambiguous times even more so, your workforce is looking to you, their leader for decisions, directions, support and safety. This means you need to have the confidence to lead and the influence to give direction and bring people along the journey to move through the unknown, to get the work done and to drive performance.

Self-leaders will have a greater sense of who they are, and therefore a greater sense of confidence in themselves and how they can lead others. They'll therefore also have greater courage spurring them on

---

12 Reardon, Kathleen K. 'Courage as a Skill'. Harvard Business Review Press, 2007.

to influence others. Furthermore, self-leaders will have strong emotional intelligence which means, among other elements, they'll have command of their internal states, self-control, adaptability, impact on others, collaboration and cooperation and trustworthiness.

What did you wish you knew about self-leadership before you stepped into your first leadership role?

It's okay to not have all the answers.

Emma Barrier
Early Childhood Education Centre Director

Snap to watch the full interview.

> So many leaders have the expectation that they must have all the answers. Day in and day out so many clues and cues reinforce that they need to have the answer to all the questions thrown at them. The truth is that no one has all the answers and those who think they do will eventually find themselves leading in a vacuum without support because others will see that leader as not wanting or needing followers. This is because no one will feel needed.
>
> Spark your self-leadership by seeking advice, inviting input, encouraging engagement, feedback and listening. You won't get it right all the time, and that's okay. It's how you handle those moments that count the most.

CHAPTER FOUR
VALUE: IT STARTS HERE!

Know your values, own your value!

At the very core of self-leadership, at the heart of influencing oneself, is knowing yourself. This includes knowing your core values, self-awareness, and it begins with emotional intelligence.

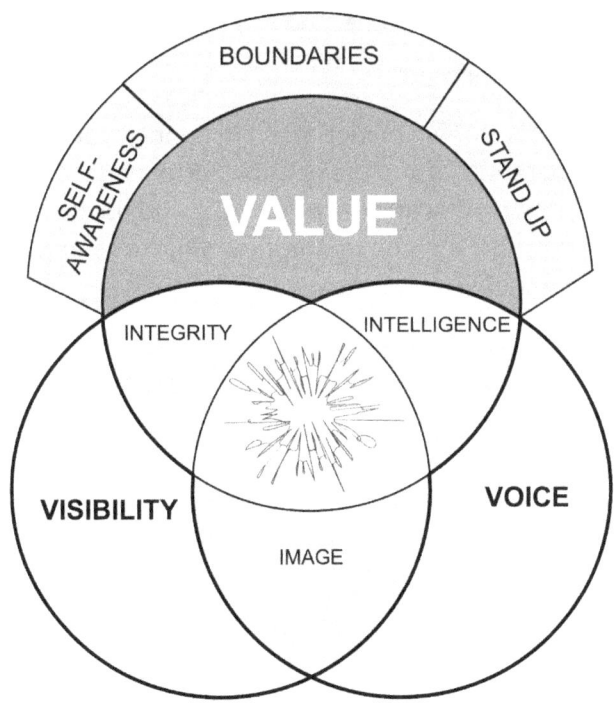

Emotional Intelligence

For strong self-leadership, self-awareness is key. The greater your self-awareness, the more equipped you will be to handle what life throws at you. This will then provide you with more options so you'll rise above the challenges you'll face. But getting here takes emotional intelligence. Tied closely to self-awareness, the work you do to strengthen your emotional intelligence will show up in every aspect of your life and leadership.

One of the world's most popular and instrumental books on emotional intelligence was written by Daniel Goleman.[13]

Emotional intelligence is a way of recognising, understanding and choosing how you think, feel and act, which shapes your understanding of yourself, your behaviours and your interactions with others.

Key to Goleman's work on emotional intelligence is that 'at best, IQ contributes about 20 percent to the factors that determine life success, which leaves 80 percent to other forces'.

As Goleman explains it:

> If your emotional abilities aren't in hand; if you don't have self-awareness, if you are not able to manage your distressing emotions, if you can't have empathy and have effective relationships, then no matter how smart you are, you are not going to get very far.[14]

When comparing someone with exceptional emotional intelligence to one who is lacking, you'll see a marked difference in a surprisingly large number of areas, including:

1. Decision-making
2. Leadership

---

[13] Goleman, Daniel, 'Emotional Intelligence: Why It Can Matter More Than IQ'. Bloomsbury: Great Britain, 1995.

[14] Goleman, Daniel, 'Emotional Intelligence: Why It Can Matter More Than IQ'. Bloomsbury: Great Britain, 1995

3. Communication
4. Sales
5. Teamwork
6. Productivity and performance
7. Customer service
8. Conflict management
9. Relationships

If someone has greater success in all of these areas, which is due in some significant part to improved emotional intelligence, then it's an easy leap to assume they'll also have greater life success and happiness. To explore this deeper, reflect on these comparisons:

	LOW EMOTIONAL INTELLIGENCE	HIGH EMOTIONAL INTELLIGENCE
Anger	Lets anger take over behaviour so they can becom e hostile in times of conflict and confrontation.	Identifies angry or frustrated feelings but can manage this emotion to aim for a win-win compromise and positive solution or resolution.
Jealousy	May be drawn into competition and 'winning'. Can feel threatened by others.	Aims for collaboration for the betterment of the team or the work, with an emphasis on abundant thinking. Will be inspired by and look for ways to learn from others success.
Relationships	Tends to have very few long-lasting, quality relationships. People may feel used by this person.	Looks for the mutual gain and growth in their relationships.

Environment	Struggles or doesn't know how or why they should 'read the room', or try to understand what others may be thinking or feeling. May need to be directly told how others are feeling.	Can effectively read verbal and non-verbal clues and cues and can adjust accordingly and show empathy.
Blame	Often won't take responsibility for mistakes, problems and difficult situations. Looks to blame others.	Will take responsibility for their own part in a problem or situation and will proactively work towards a solution.
Feeling	Tends to feel misunderstood and unappreciated.	Has the ability to flex and adjust to different situations and different people.

Emotional intelligence is divided into four areas of focus:

Self-Recognition: includes self-awareness, intrapersonal communication, self-acceptance and confidence and being able to identify one's emotions.

Self-Management: includes discipline and self-control, integrity and being trustworthy, tapping into one's motivation and initiative to achieve goals and being flexible and adaptable.

Social Recognition: includes having the ability to perceive what's happening in any given situation, empathy and sensitivity to others and good interpersonal communication.

Social Management: influence, negotiation and conflict management, teamwork and collaboration, building and maintaining relationships, leadership and being able to get along with others.

These four areas are interrelated and are influenced by, and can influence, your values.

When you have high emotional intelligence, you will have a clear understanding of your value and contribution to the work, the organisation, the team and leadership.

Your Values

The more self-aware and the more emotionally intelligent you are the more equipped you'll be to perform in alignment with your values. Being clear about what your values are helps you hold boundaries, which in turn helps maintain respectful relationships.

Having a clear sense of your values helps ensure you are living an authentic life. Your values guide your decisions. They are like a lighthouse for directing your decisions.

When my signature was forged by my boss in the early days of my career, those were anxious and then later, angry moments. I wasn't thinking of my values but they were definitely informing my feelings and thinking. I have a deep sense of justice!

With known and aligned values you are best placed to gain clarity when you see them in action in your everyday life. Have you ever known someone who says they value hard work but they are the last to pitch in and help out? Or they complain about having too much work and will constantly seek out short cuts and ways to off load their own work? (Note: I'm not averse to short cuts if they are not at the expense of quality and the impact on others.)

In the self-leadership workshop, I often ask participants to write down their top five to 10 values. In every workshop, to date, there is always at least one person who will struggle to identify what their values are and a few who can identify just a few values. But identifying your values is a vital part of understanding your value and what you can offer the world.

Practice: Identify your values

Before shifting into the strategies for exceptional self-leadership for the value segment, take time to identify your values. Values are what you believe are most important for you and how you live and work.

Using the word lists below, circle the words that resonate with you. Do not overthink your choices. If you think of a value you have that's not on the list, write it down.

Abundance
Acceptance of diversity
Activism
Advancement
Adventure
Aesthetics
Ambition
Animal rights
Art
Attention to detail
Authenticity
Balance
Beauty
Be kind to neighbours
Calmness
Challenge
Challenging myself
Change and variety

Charity
Clarity
Classical thinking
Collaboration
Colour
Community
Compassion
Competence
Competition
Country values
Courage
Creativity
Cultural diversity
Curiosity
Decisiveness
Democracy
Emotional availability
Empathy
Equality
Excitement

Experimentation
Expertise
Fashion
Fairness and social justice
Family
Feminism
Financial security
Flexibility
Forgiveness
Frankness
Freedom of choice
Friendship
Fun
Generosity
Global awareness
Global peace
Growth
Happiness/ positive attitude
Harmony

Having a say/ voice
Having dreams
Health
Help others
Help society
Honesty
Honour
Humour
Imagination and creativity
Independence
Influencing people
Inner harmony
Innovation
Inspiring others
Integrity
Intellectual status
Intelligence
Kindness
Knowledge

Laughter
Leadership
Learning
Leisure
Literature
Living your dreams
Love for myself
Love for others
Making a difference
Making decisions
Massive wealth
Moral fulfilment
Music
Natural living
Nature
Open communication
Opening myself to love
Optimism

Passion
Patriotism
Persistence
Personal expression
Personal growth
Perspective
Physical challenge
Play
Pleasure
Positive attitude
Positiveness
Power and authority
Precision
Professionalism
Protecting the environment
Quality of life
Quiet times
Recognition

Relationship with spouse
Reliability
Respect
Results
Risk taking
Security
Self-control
Self-respect
Sensuality
Smiling at strangers
Spiritual enlightenment
Spirituality
Spontaneity
Stability
Standing up for yourself
Storytelling
Style
Sunlight

Support
Supportive friendship
Taking care of myself
Taking responsibility
Taking risks
The big picture
Thinking time
Tidiness
Time freedom
Tolerance
Tranquillity
Trust
Trustworthiness
Understanding
Wonder and awe
Worker's rights
Workmanship

Values not on the list but that are your values:

_____
_____
_____
_____
_____

Now that you've selected a range of values it's time to group them into categories that makes sense to you. In other words, which values align with each other? Write the groupings into the table below. Aim for no more than five categories or groups of values.

Group One	Group Two	Group Three	Group Four	Group Five

Now look at each group and pick a word that would describe that group of values; for example, if you picked the values *justice, ethics, loyalty, trust, democracy*, then you might pick the word *fairness*. It's important that you pick a word that makes sense to you and that truly sums of the group of values for you.

Group One	Group Two	Group Three	Group Four	Group Five
Label:	Label:	Label:	Label:	Label:

As this is all about self-leadership and self-leadership is about influencing oneself, the next step is to bring these values to life, creating actionable drivers to influence your actions. To do this add a verb to each value.

For example:

> If justice is one of your values, then you might add *protect justice* or *dispense justice*.
>
> If mental health is one of your values, then you might add *promote mental health* or *maintain mental health*.
>
> If money is one of your values, then you might add *save money*, *make money* or *earn money*.

Consider posting these value phrases where you can see them often, especially in easily accessible places for times when you may feel like your values are challenged.

The Three Value Strategies

As you progress deeper into this part of the book, you'll notice that you've already undertaken a simple strategy. Call that one a bonus. I didn't want to share the next three strategies without first discussing emotional intelligence and doing the all-important core inner values work.

The three strategies that you embark on now will help improve your self-awareness and confidence and help you to better understand your value.

> We cannot think of being acceptable to others until we first have proven acceptable to ourselves.
>
> —Malcolm X

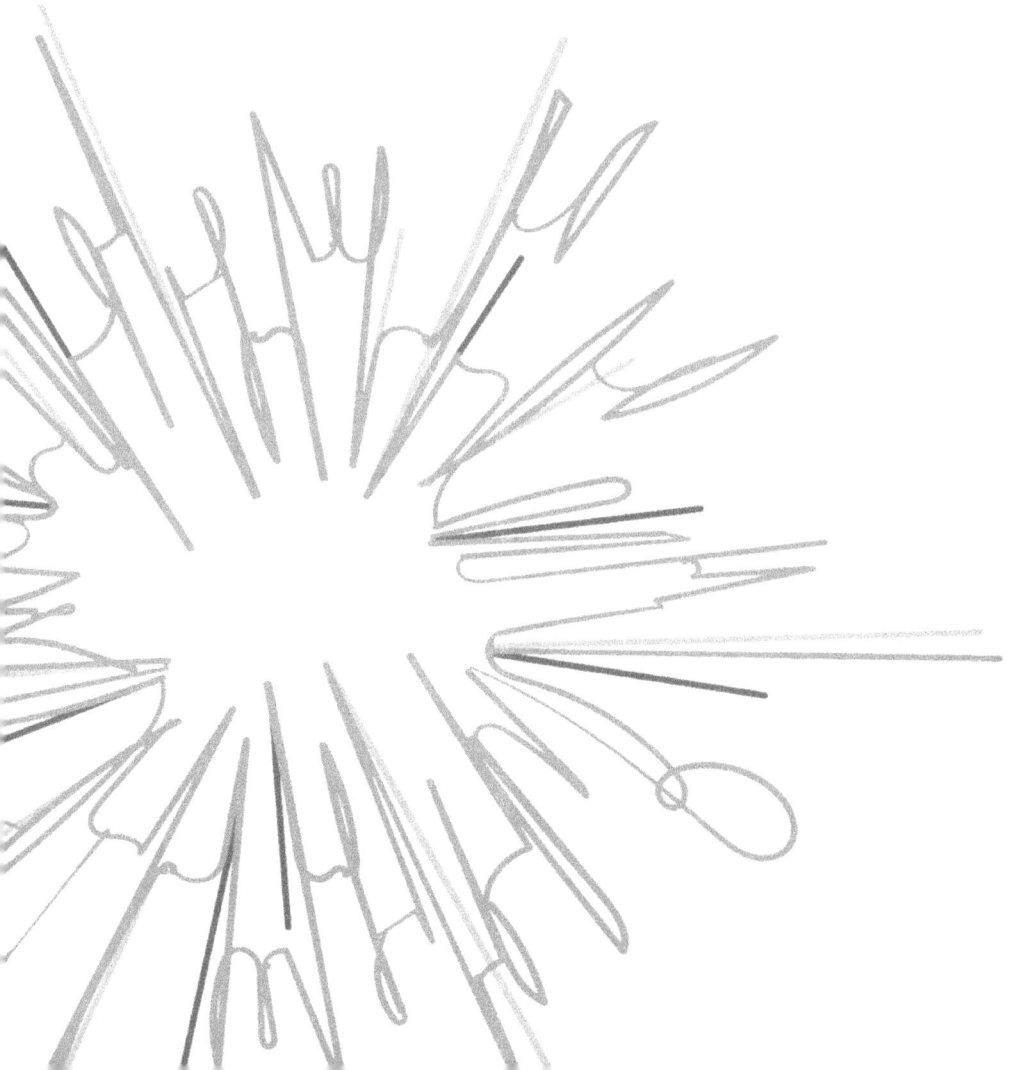

What did you wish you knew about self-leadership before you stepped into your first leadership role?

The first thing is that it's really hard. It's okay to have all of the dramas, the ups and the downs, and lose your confidence, that's all part of the journey. And I think the second part is that everybody is really actually very motivated. I've never found anybody, even in some really awful corporate environments and toxic teams, I've never really found anyone who doesn't want to self-lead and do better.

And I really do believe that inside everybody there is that, that little thing where they go, "Oh, I could do better. I want to do better. I want to learn something new, maybe I'm wrong, maybe I should be curious."

And sometimes it takes a lot of time, but everybody has got that spark.

Rowena Samaraweera
Customer Experience Design Lead

Snap to watch the full interview.

Rowena reminds leaders that life is not always a bed of roses. There will be challenges and there will be times when your confidence will waiver. Tapping into your self-leadership will help you regain your confidence quickly, allowing you to bounce back sooner.

Like you, people want to do well. Very few people actually don't want to do well. As a leader, you can spark your own self-leadership by keeping that front of mind. It will help you to help yourself and others to rise to and overcome challenges and be ready to take opportunities.

CHAPTER FIVE

SELF-AWARENESS: KNOW THYSELF—KNOW THY VALUE!

STRATEGY ONE

One of the most effective ways to learn about yourself is to ask for feedback from those who know you well. Everyone has blind spots – the lack of perception or awareness about yourself in a certain area – and decreasing your blind spots leads to greater self-awareness.

Practice: What's in a word or 25?

Take a moment and ponder these questions:

- Think about the person you aspire to be.
- Who are the people you admire?
- What are their characteristics and traits?
- What do they do that makes you admire them?
- How are you similar to them and how do you differ?

When I run this self-awareness activity in workshops and executive coaching sessions not only do leaders gain a deeper sense of self, they also get a boost to their confidence and motivation.

25 words, give or take!

Write down five words you would want used to describe you. These might be words that you would want the world to use to describe you, your nature, your leadership or your character.

1. _____

2. _____

3. _____

4. _____

5. _____

Now write down the names of five people who know you quite well. Consider selecting people from different parts of your life. For example, you might select a family member, a community member, a close friend or two and a work colleague.

1. _____

2. _____

3. _____

4. _____

5. _____
   _____

The next step is to email those five people asking them to describe you in five words. You can use the following text. Feel free to vary the wording to suit you, but please maintain the integrity of the exercise, that is, asking for five words.

> *Hi.*
>
> *I'm doing a leadership and self-awareness exercise and I would appreciate your help. Could you please share with me five words that you'd use to describe me?*
>
> *Thank you.*

As the responses come in you can complete the table below:

NAME	WORDS

You can ask more people if you'd like, especially if some on your original list don't respond.

You may find that some people will offer more than five words, and that's okay. Leaders often receive a quick reply of, 'Only five words?' Hence why this strategy is called *25 Words, Give or Take!*

Once you have approximately 25 words, compare those to the words you that you had written down to describe yourself.

Looking over these two lists, reflect on the following:

1. How similar are the two lists?
2. Do others see you in a similar way to how you see yourself?
3. With those that are similar, how does that make you feel about how you are seen?
4. With those that are different, how does that make you feel about how you are seen?

It's time to challenge yourself. What gaps do you see between your list and how others see you? Write your thoughts below.

_____
_____
_____
_____

What one change to your behaviour or actions can you start doing now to close that gap? Write your thoughts below.

_____
_____
_____
_____

Who you are and who you want to be is your choice. Sometimes your intentions won't align with how others see your behaviour. In fact, it's very common for each of us to judge others by the behaviour we see but to judge ourselves by our intentions. This strategy is a great feedback exercise to help your behaviours align with who you aspire to be.

To date, whenever I've run this activity in workshops and executive coaching, no one has received all negative words. In fact, most have received far more positive words than they expected.

If a leader did receive all negative responses then that would no doubt be a bitter pill to swallow. But the feedback could prove invaluable for improving and increasing their self-awareness, development and self-leadership. By reflecting on the questions above as well as their behaviours and relationships with their respondents they could begin to make sense of why their lists would be so different.

As Australian author, Daniel Chidiac, says, 'Being self-aware is not the absence of mistakes, but the ability to learn and correct them'. Any differences that initially challenge you can be seen as an opportunity to learn from both an emotional intelligence perspective as well as from the specific behaviour or leadership aspect the word evokes or relates to.

What did you wish you knew about self-leadership before you stepped into your first leadership role?

The number one thing that I learned is the relevance of your why, your purpose.

Jo Sainsbury
Coal Train Driver & Advocate

Snap to watch the full interview.

Your purpose or your why is linked to your core values. Your core values represent the things that mean the most to you. Think about your career choices, life choices, partner and friend choices… what are the common values that emerge? How does this highlight your purpose? Your why?

Spark your self-leadership by reflecting on your core values.

Expand your self-awareness and watch your confidence grow!
—Sally Foley-Lewis

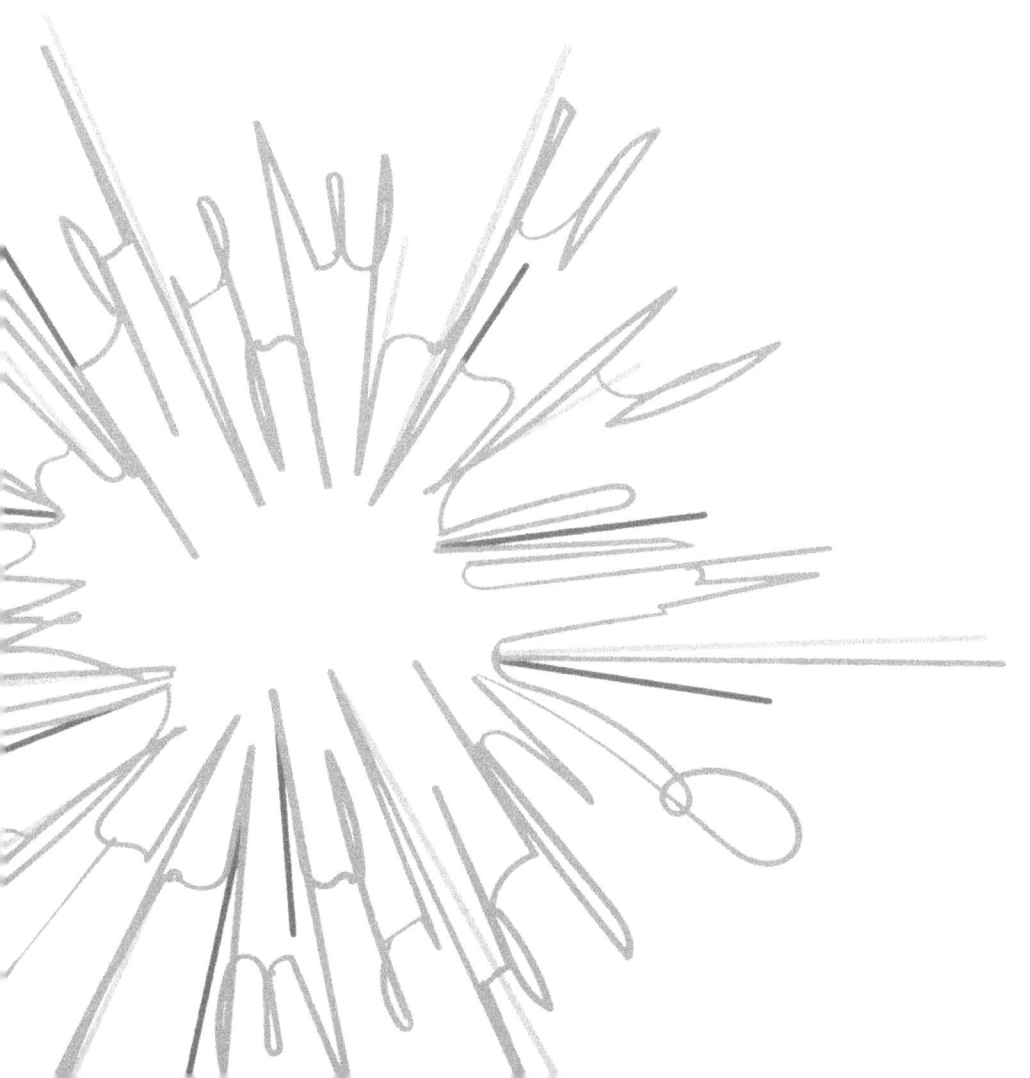

Feedback

It's unknown who said, 'an inability to tolerate feedback is an inability to allow yourself personal growth'. But regardless of its origin, this is a succinct rationale for the value of feedback to strengthen self-leadership by expanding our self-awareness.

Actively seeking feedback gives you insight into your strengths, weaknesses, blind spots and even opportunities. With feedback you can work on your skills, knowledge and mindset so that you have greater confidence and the capability to handle what comes your way. At the end of the day, feedback helps you understand yourself deeper.

Validation versus Feedback

When I created my very first product, the Management Success Cards, I was so excited. And I was totally in love with the result. I presented the cards to my then mastermind group—it's first public viewing. But as I was preparing to present, I also had to admit to myself where my emotions were. So as I showed my cards, I asked that no one give me any feedback that day. Instead, I asked them to simply validate the product and me and tell me how great it was.

Everyone giggled with empathy with me. But it worked. Once I felt validated, and I had gotten over the very first public viewing of the card set, I reached out to each mastermind member and asked for their honest feedback, reassuring them I was ready to hear anything and everything I needed to help improve what I created.

This highlights three key points to remember when seeking feedback for greater self-awareness:

1. Consider who you seek feedback from. Pick feedback givers who have your best interests at heart and will tell you what you need to hear, and not just what you want to hear. This flows into picking your mentors wisely, too (see strategy eight for more on this).

2. When you are on the receiving end of poorly delivered feedback, especially from a boss, focus on the content more than the delivery. Ask questions to make sure you're clear about the intent of the feedback. Look past how they are delivering the message and aim to understand what is the most important part for your self-leadership and professional development.
3. Be clear that you are seeking feedback rather than validation. Very few people ignore validation. Even if it's not easy to accept a compliment, it's still nice to receive. However, mere validation is not that helpful for expanding your self-awareness and growth.

Feedback is Nothing Without Action

After finally summoning the courage to reach out to someone I admired greatly to ask their guidance, I then asked how I could repay him for his time and wisdom. He wisely said, 'Implement! Thank me by putting the information I shared into action'.

And it's important to remember to always thank your feedback giver. It's not always easy to give feedback but your gratitude for their effort to help and support you will go a long way. Also, share how you will implement, or have implemented, their advice. It will demonstrate how you valued them and their wisdom and care for you.

Practice: Self-Feedback

Start with your own self-reflection. You can use the following questions to undertake a regular review of where you're at or when a situation arises that challenges you:

1. What happened?

_____

_____

_____

2. How did that/this go?

___

3. Was the outcome expected?

___

4. What, if anything, surprised me? (My strengths, behaviours, etc.)

___

5. What, if anything, challenged me? (My weaknesses, interactions, etc.)

___

6. Where were my confidence levels throughout that/this? Why?

___

7. How do I really feel about _____? (Even if I don't share these feelings with anyone else.)

_____
_____
_____

8. What would I do differently?

_____
_____
_____

9. What will I try next time?

_____
_____
_____

10. Who can I ask for help when I try this differently?

_____
_____
_____

External Feedback

There are many ways to get feedback. And we've discussed some of them. But another great way is through specific assessments such as an emotional intelligence assessment.

Assessments will give you the feedback you need to make changes that can help you to grow. And when done with an accredited provider, that expert can debrief the results with you and help you develop a plan for taking action. When I work with my clients on these assessments we are always able to make strong inroads into their growth and success.

A common form of feedback that's executed during leadership programs is the 360-degree feedback. This aims to solicit feedback from direct reports, peers and senior leaders so that the individual has data from people below, beside and above them (hence, 360 degree). There are versions of this feedback that are extensive and laborious, anonymous or semi-anonymous, online or pen and paper. But however they are accomplished, they can be incredibly valuable exercises when executed well.

If actively seeking feedback is new, start small and build from there.

Practice: Active External Feedback

1. Identify three to five people who know you well and that you trust will actively engage in a feedback conversation.
2. Think about the area of your life where you'd like feedback, such as skills, self-awareness, leadership or self-leadership. Write out five questions that are specific to that area or topic.
3. Reach out to the people on your list and ask them to consider the questions and if they could meet with you to provide their perspective on you in relation to your questions.

The following copy may be helpful:

> *Hello (Feedback Giver Name),*
>
> *I'm undertaking a professional development exercise and I'd value your feedback.*
>
> *Below are five items about key self-leadership and leadership principles I'd like you to reflect on with respect to me and my level of competency.*

You can provide your feedback by answering the following questions and I'd really appreciate meeting with you to go through the responses with you.

Thank you,
Your Name

Here are some example questions you could use:

You can download a copy of this at https://bit.ly/SampleFeedbackSPARK

Self-Awareness

Please rate me on *self-awareness*:

	Among the bottom 10%	Among the bottom third	Typical	Among the leading third	Among the leading 10%
Keeps control of their emotions and behaviour, even when involved in high-pressure situations					
Is highly ethical					
Acts professionally					
Learns from their mistakes					

Please provide any additional feedback you have about this area:

_____
_____
_____
_____
_____

Drive for Results

Please rate me in terms of *drive for results*:

	Among the bottom 10%	Among the bottom third	Typical	Among the leading third	Among the leading 10%
Is focused on the needs of the customer					
Is a problem solver					

Please provide any additional feedback you have about this area:

_____
_____
_____
_____
_____

Leadership

Please rate my proficiency in *leadership*:

	Among the bottom 10%	Among the bottom third	Typical	Among the leading third	Among the leading 10%
Inspires continuous growth and learning in others					
Handles conflict in an appropriate manner					
Takes initiative to solve problems					
Motivates others to reach their goals					

Please provide any additional feedback you have about my leadership:

_____
_____
_____
_____
_____
_____
_____
_____

Communication

Please rate my ability with interpersonal *communication*:

	Among the bottom 10%	Among the bottom third	Typical	Among the leading third	Among the leading 10%
Communicates openly/effectively with others					
Is open and receptive to feedback/seeks out feedback					

Please provide any additional feedback you have about my interpersonal communication skills:

_____
_____
_____
_____

Teamwork

Please rate my ability with *teamwork*:

	Among the bottom 10%	Among the bottom third	Typical	Among the leading third	Among the leading 10%
Works well in a team					

Gives constructive and helpful feedback					
Treats others with respect					
Responds constructively to the mistakes of others					
Is open to change and innovation					

Please provide any additional feedback you have about this area:

_____
_____
_____
_____

Share a concrete example of something I do well:

_____
_____
_____
_____

Share a concrete example of something I could improve:

_____
_____
_____
_____

Being entirely honest with oneself
is a good exercise.
—Sigmund Freud

CHAPTER SIX

BOUNDARIES: GOOD FENCES MAKE GOOD NEIGHBOURS

STRATEGY TWO

I worked for a time at The Duke of Edinburgh's Award program, and as a safety measure our CEO had a pager. This was the type of device where you would get a beep and then you'd have to call the number on the screen. Today, pagers are non-existent but even back then it was an old-fashioned version.

The reason for having a pager was because a component of the youth program involved young people going on outdoor expeditions. This would include hiking and camping and all manner of outdoor activities. The pager was so the CEO could be contacted in case of an emergency should any of the young people find themselves in any form of distress. In the event of an emergency the young people would contact the relevant emergency or civil services first, and the CEO would be contacted soon after to handle the more administrative (and political) tasks.

It wasn't until I became the CEO of the program that I learned the chairman of the board, Alan, would page the CEO at approximately 6:30am most weekday mornings wanting to discuss issues, projects or opportunities. The first time I was paged you can image my fright when I thought there had been an emergency with some of our young people in the program. I rang the number listed on the pager only to be confused by Alan answering the call to say he wanted to chat about the latest minutes of the board meeting and the international news for the program.

My predecessor hadn't informed me that Alan used the pager as an alarm-clock-cum-call-me prompter … regularly! I wondered if the previous CEO hadn't seemed to mind. I pondered whether he had clear or any boundaries for the use of emergency equipment or he didn't have a clear boundary for his work and personal time.

When I approached Alan about his use of the pager he hadn't been aware that the device was only for emergencies. While he was somewhat apologetic about the mis-use he still wanted to reach me on his terms and on his timeframe. I reminded him of my standard work hours and told him that while I would always respond to an emergency at any time of the day, operational matters would be handled in standard work hours.

Was this easy for me to say? Not entirely. It took me some time to script out what I wanted to say and how I wanted to say it so that it would be received in the best possible way. Was I nervous when I approached Alan to have this conversation? Absolutely! And was he accepting and happy with what I had to say? Not exactly.

Alan asked for my mobile number and I declined to provide it as this was still early mobile phone days and our devices were not a standard part of our work equipment. I informed him that even with an employer-provided mobile phone I would not respond to out-of-hours operational calls.

It took him a few days to, let's diplomatically say, digest my setting of this boundary. But once he could see I was not going to budge he adjusted. When his term ended he did mention to me privately that he realised he hadn't considered the impact he had on the CEO role, though he did want the last word by saying that he was operating from a drive to get as much done as possible.

For me, this was an invaluable lesson in boundaries. If I let the behaviour continue as per my predecessor, then I know I would have struggled to maintain a positive relationship with Alan. I would have reached frustration very quickly and our working relationship would have suffered. As it was it only took a few days of awkwardness and then we got back into the day-to-day of our respective jobs, working well together.

If I had not taken the time to think about what and how to say what I needed to say, or if I had just blurted out my frustration, I would have really damaged the relationship, or even jeopardised my job.

While I was nervous, and while I couldn't guarantee how he would respond or react to my boundary, it was a conversation that still had to happen. I had no idea if he would agree to my boundary setting, but I knew I was worthy of protecting my time and it was worth thinking of the long-term quality of our relationship.

The quality of my relationship with Alan had a very real connection with my employment status and in those kinds of cases it can be challenging to set and hold boundaries. It's always more difficult with those who are more senior or whose good opinion you don't want to lose.

American psychologist and author, Adam Grant sums it up well when he challenges us to keep in mind, 'It's impossible to please everyone. The question is whether you're disappointing the right people. Part of setting healthy boundaries is deciding who you're willing to let down—and who has the right to make you feel guilty. Not everyone deserves power over your emotions'.

Boundaries are not new. The phrase, 'good fences make good neighbours' is traced as far back as 1914. Even Benjamin Franklin, one of the founding fathers of the United States, is known to have said, 'Love thy neighbour, yet don't pull down your hedge'.

A boundary is quite simply a line that marks a limit!

However, in Frost's poem, *Mending Wall*, which reiterates this phrase, it's actually used to show how walls can keep people out of our lives with negative consequences. And it's true that too tight or too rigid boundaries may lead to you missing out on opportunities. You could be keeping others at a distance who could be a help or support to you. You may be perceived as aloof or detached from others. And you may even have fewer relationships because others may not find it easy to build a relationship with you.

Conversely, boundaries that are too loose or too open may mean that you find yourself getting too close to other people's problems or drama, oversharing your own personal information, struggling to say no to requests or even feeling drawn into seeking others approval, whether out of a desire to please or because you fear their rejection.

Boundaries can be personal, physical or psychological. But regardless of their type, when it comes to the boundaries you may have, they could impact many areas of your life such as:

- Personal or physical space
- Time
- Culture and/or religion
- Ethics
- Possessions
- Sexuality
- Emotions and thoughts

When you identify, set and hold a healthy boundary you will find that this helps conserve your emotional and physical energy. In the case of Alan and the pager, once I set and held the boundary, I felt as though my energy was no longer being zapped away or re-directed to an issue of frustration but could be directed to the work I needed to do at the time I needed to do it.

Benefits of Boundaries

Healthy boundaries can have many benefits. They will help boost your self-esteem and self-worth because you have put in place a measure that will protect your values and your needs. They will also give you the skills, experience and courage to respect your own and others' boundaries. And it will give you more agency—more control and confidence over your actions and the consequences.

Practice: Identify a Boundary

Have you ever been in a situation where you felt completely zapped, drained or stressed or where you found that you've got a knot in your stomach or felt like crying?

Name a situation where you've felt this?

_____
_____
_____
_____

Reflect on that situation, taking into consideration what was said, how things were said and how you responded versus how you may have wanted to respond. (For example, maybe you said yes when you would have preferred to say no.) Write down your thoughts below.

_____
_____
_____
_____

What caused your feelings of upset? Was it more the situation or the people? Or was it a meeting, event or project that caused or triggered the uncomfortable feeling?

_____
_____
_____
_____

This reflection should give you insight into the situations, words, actions or events where you would benefit from setting a healthy boundary so you can handle them better. Or, better yet, not have to deal with them at all. Even if the situation is unavoidable it can give you clarity on how the situation can be handled.

Identification is the first step. Setting boundaries is the next step.

Practice: Setting Boundaries

A simple strategy for setting boundaries is to finish the following sentences.

> You may not …
> Others may not …
> People may not …

For example:

> … hug me unless I say it's okay.
>
> … gossip to me about others when those people are not there to defend themselves.
>
> … add meetings into the blocked off time in my calendar without asking me first.

_____
_____
_____
_____
_____
_____
_____

It is okay for me to protect myself by …

For example:

> … not replying to emails out of office hours.
> … not answering phone calls out of office hours.
> … closing the office door.

_____
_____
_____
_____
_____

> It's okay for me to ask for…
> I'm entitled to ask for…
> I have the right to ask for…

For example:

> …time off.
> … help.
> … clarification on an issue.
> … privacy.
> … feedback.

_____
_____
_____
_____
_____

How do you feel after finishing these sentences?

_____
_____
_____
_____
_____
_____
_____

It's okay if these are not perfect. See your statements as a first draft and not necessarily right or wrong. They are your boundaries and you can tweak them as you continue to spark your self-leadership and especially your self-awareness.

The more you work on these the clearer you'll become about what your boundaries need to be. If I wasn't clear with Alan, and if he didn't understand exactly the boundaries I was setting, he would have continued to page me and continued to expect me to be available at unreasonable hours of the day. If I was unclear it would be akin to being unkind because it would have negatively affected our relationship. I may have inadvertently blown up at him and it would most certainly have been my fault, not his. He would simply have been operating according to what he believed was acceptable behaviour.

What did you wish you knew about self-leadership before you stepped into your first leadership role?

It's not possible to be all things to all people.

Josh Grocke
**Head of Account Management,
Flight Centre Business Travel**

Snap to watch
the full interview.

Remembering Adam Grants quote, 'It's impossible to please everyone. The question is whether you're disappointing the right people. Part of setting healthy boundaries is deciding who you're willing to let down— and who has the right to make you feel guilty. Not everyone deserves power over your emotions'. Josh Grocke has this knowledge engrained in his leadership.

Spark your self-leadership by strengthening your boundary setting. Start small and practice with smaller or less critical boundaries.

CHAPTER SEVEN

STAND UP: STAND UP FOR YOURSELF, EVEN IF NO ONE IS ON YOUR SIDE.

STRATEGY THREE

Your self-worth is influenced by your values and emotional intelligence, as well as your confidence and conviction in the authenticity of your feelings. It shows up in how you regard and care for yourself and for others.

It also shows up in how you approach and handle your work. If you're not clear on your own needs and feelings, you can be easily distracted and find yourself overwhelmed more than you are focused. When you're overwhelmed you'll struggle to stay on the course to goal achievement. This also means that it can be easier for others to take advantage of your time and expertise, intentionally or otherwise. All this results in situations where it's more difficult for you to stand up for yourself.

Growing up, my mum once said to me, 'Darling, never get off your own stage for anyone else'. It took me a little while to understand exactly what she meant. But now my interpretation is that I need to stand in my own power, follow my dreams and goals, be true to my own feelings and be sure to have my needs met. If I lose sight of myself to follow the dreams and needs of another then I may never stand up for myself. I risk losing myself and who I am.

In leadership workshops, when talking about standing up for yourself, I often hear leaders say:

> *'I have to stand my ground and not let them push me around.'*
> *'It's about getting what I want.'*
> *'It's being blunt so I won't get walked all over.'*

These statements are often said with a brusque tone. It always makes me curious about what has happened for the leaders to feel this way and to speak with such force or angst.

Standing up for yourself is not only about making sure you don't get pushed around or taken advantage of. It's also about getting your needs met, though certainly not at the expense or harm, disrespect or disregard of others. Standing up for yourself requires strong self-awareness and values alignment in combination with quality intra- and interpersonal relationships.

When it comes to intrapersonal, or internal, relationships, it's about understanding your value and what standing up for yourself means to you. This is where the values exercise and learning to identify and set boundaries stands you in good stead.

'No' Doesn't Need Excuses, But Alternatives Can Help

Saying no can often be enough to let others know where you stand. However, sometimes people slip into giving a list of excuses as to why they won't or can't fulfil a request. Rambling off excuses tends to undermine your confidence as well as diminish the confidence others will have in you.

It's okay to simply say no. You don't need to offer any reason for your no ever. But in many situations it can feel rude or dismissive to simply say no. In those cases, there are some alternatives you could use which will help you give the 'no' you want to deliver, without diminishing your confidence:

'Thank you for thinking of me for this, however I will respectfully say no at this time.'

'Thank you for thinking of me for this opportunity, however I will need to say no at this time.'

'Thank you, but I will say no at this time.'

If you want to say no and be helpful and redirect the request you can consider a version of 'not me, not now, not that'. For example:

Not me: 'Thank you for thinking of me, however I'm not the right person for this. I believe Bob would have some great insights and could help you.'

Not now: 'Thank you for inviting me to work on this, however I've got a big project on right now / I've got XYZ priority right now. I can help <when>.'

Not that: 'This sounds interesting but I'm curious if you've considered ABC? That is something I would be better suited to help with and I believe it would give you the 123 result I think you're after.'

Stand up with A.A.R.E.A.™

Another version of standing up for yourself, which avoids the rambling excuses and allows you to continue to hold your personal power, is to follow A.A.R.E.A.™

- A—**Acknowledge** the request.
- A—Give your **answer**. Or,
- A—**Advocate** and state your case
- R—Share the single **reason** for your answer
- E—Provide an objective piece of **evidence** or an **example** to back up your reason.
- A—Re-**affirm** your answer.

Example 1: You've been asked to take on a new project which is a new venture for the company and so has many unknown elements. You can see that the different components will require you to undertake retraining and new skills training on top of your current workload while also starting the new project. The demand is too high and it's not an area of expertise you ever wanted to explore.

There is no doubt more than one way to address this request, but here's one example:

- Acknowledge – Thank you for considering me for this new venture.
- Answer – I will respectfully decline the opportunity to lead the project.
- Reason – I can see areas within the new project that will call for skills I don't have. That will mean training. I'm not interested in this area of expertise or following down that pathway.
- Evidence – As an example, phase two calls for skills in A and B. I would need to attend training in these areas before embarking on that phase, which would cause a significant delay.
- Affirm – Again, thank you but I will say no.

Example 2: You are attending a virtual team meeting when your boss started announcing a brand new project the organisation is taking on. As you listen you realise the project is a perfect fit for your skillset. You even have some capacity in your workload so you could probably make it work. It sounds so exciting!

A colleague private messages you to say congratulations as they also assume you'll be heading the project. This indicates that others also see you as the right choice. And then your boss announces someone else will be heading the project. You feel as though you didn't even get a second, let alone first, thought.

- Acknowledge – This project looks like an amazing opportunity for the organisation.
- Advocate – This project suits my skillset perfectly so I'd like to put myself forward to lead / participate in this project or understand

why I might not have had the opportunity. Your feedback would be helpful.
- Reason – I have X, Y, Z skills and A, B, C experience that would suit this project and I am confident I could make it a success.
- Evidence – My experience on project K called for my skills in X, Y, Z and we were able to complete that project on time with the value add of N, all while coming in under budget.
- Affirm – Are you open to discussing this further?

You may still not get the opportunity. However, you will walk away from that exchange with more confidence in yourself because you stood up for yourself. The decision maker will see you as more confident and may reconsider you for future participation or put you in line for the next opportunity.

Practice: Standing Up For Yourself

Think of the last time you were asked to do something, were disregarded or were left to feel dismissed and you did not stand up for yourself?

What happened?

_____
_____
_____

If you were to be confronted by that situation again today, using A.A.R.E.A.™ what would you say:

_____
_____
_____

Acknowledge:
_____
_____
_____
_____

Answer / Advocate:
_____
_____
_____
_____

Reason:
_____
_____
_____
_____

Evidence:
_____
_____
_____
_____

Affirm / Re-affirm:
_____
_____
_____

The Power of Assertiveness

The need to stand up for yourself can come from a range of situations. But the best way to successfully handle each situation is by being assertive.

Assertiveness is based on a theory of personal responsibility and an awareness and respect of the rights of other people. Being assertive means being honest with yourself and others. It's about having the ability to directly say what it is you want, need or feel, but not at the expense of other people. And it's having confidence in yourself and being positive, while at the same time understanding other people's points of view.

There are many benefits of being assertive:

- Increases your self-esteem
- Improves your self-leadership
- Improves close working relationships
- You gain greater confidence in others
- You save time and energy
- You improve your ability to negotiate more effectively
- You increase the chance of everyone winning

More Ways to Stand Up for Yourself

The following are some common situations where you can feel your confidence waiver but actually where standing up for yourself can amplify your confidence and courage.

Personal Questions

You don't have to answer questions you feel are too personal or an invasion of your privacy. For many years an in-law of mine would ask me why my husband and I hadn't started a family. It was none of his business and I would simply respond with, 'I'd rather not speak about that'. He did ask a few times but it didn't take long before he left the topic alone.

Not Responding Immediately

When given a request it can feel like you've been put on the spot and need to respond immediately. So long as it's not life-threatening brain or heart surgery then you can simply say, 'I'd like to think about this, I'll get back to you <when>'.

Excuse yourself

At a networking function a lady made a bee-line for me. As she walked towards me she extended her hand ready for a hand shake. Initially I felt relief as I'd never been to that type of function before. She introduced herself, took just enough time to hear my name and then dived into her sales pitch for her product, including telling me how much I needed her product and how it helped cure her cancer. She didn't know me at all. It was awkward, to say the least.

As soon as I noticed her take a breath in her monologue, I said, 'Please excuse me I need to use the bathroom'. And I walked away.

I didn't feel bad about interrupting or walking away as I suspected she didn't see me at all. She only saw a sales target.

Stand Tall

While you're excusing yourself and walking away make sure you're standing tall. American social psychologist, Amy Cuddy researched how the power of posture impacts on how we feel.

The power pose is an expansive pose—standing up, hands on hips or arms stretched out, feet somewhat apart. Think of the pose superheros make, such as Wonder Woman. Cuddy suggests that by standing in a powerful stance you can make yourself feel more powerful[15]. Essentially, Amy found that people who put themselves into a power pose and make themselves bigger will feel more powerful and are more assertive and confident. She prescribes holding a power pose for two minutes which will shift your presence and confidence.

In the case of excusing myself and walking away, I prepared to walk away by taking a deep breath, standing tall with shoulders back, and lifting my chin.

You're not for everyone

As soon as you realise that you're not for everyone, you will feel more confident in owning who you are. Some people will simply not understand or like you. Nor will you understand or like everyone. We can however respect differences and value those differences. After all, they can provide for interesting learning and help expand our world views and perspectives, hence improving one's self-leadership.

The first sale is to yourself

When I first heard Peter Cook, a mentor of mine from Thought Leaders, say 'the first sale is to yourself' it was a light bulb moment. The first sale is to yourself! While he was talking about believing in your product or service from a pure business sense, it one hundred percent applies to standing up for yourself. You must believe in yourself first to be able to stand up for yourself.

---

15 Elsesser, Kim. 'The Debate On Power Posing Continues: Here's Where We Stand'. *Forbes*. October 2, 2020. Accessed at https://www.forbes.com/sites/kimelsesser/2020/10/02/the-debate-on-power-posing-continues-heres-where-we-stand/?sh=26a881c7202e.

When you stand up for yourself,
you are standing up for everyone who will
follow your positive example.
—Doreen Virtue

What did you wish you knew about self-leadership before you stepped into your first leadership role?

What somebody says to you, says more about them than it does about you.

Sarah Markey-Hamm
CEO, ICMS

Snap to watch
the full interview.

I agree with this statement and would build on it by suggesting that what somebody says to you may also be well intended feedback, so it's a choice you need to make about how you take those messages on board and how you will respond and act moving forward.

You can spark your self-leadership by ensuring you avoid reacting to what people say to you, reflect on what intention may be in play with their message, and determine how to use the information to continue your own self-leadership and leadership journey.

CHAPTER EIGHT

VOICE: THE RIGHT MESSAGE, IN THE RIGHT TONE, AT THE RIGHT TIME!

Words Can Build or Break

At a conference I was speaking at there was a caricaturist offering free caricatures for conference participants and attendees. As I sat down, I jokingly said, 'Just capture the one chin, won't you?' Without even the smallest change to his posture, or missing a breath or a beat, he responded in a calm and kind tone, 'No need to point out what others don't see.'

What a gift and what wise words!

Choose Your Words Wisely

The inner voice and the spoken word of the self-leader are confident, positive, clear and calm. They are used to build people up, not break them down. And it doesn't take much to do just that. By way of example, the caricaturist only said one sentence to me, but it's one that impacted me greatly and that I've never forgotten. His one line woke me up to my own self-talk.

How you talk to yourself impacts how you speak with others. As a leader you're in a powerful position to impact people every single day with your words. And it's your responsibility to use them wisely, starting with your self-talk.

Your values will drive how you speak with others but they will also drive how you speak about yourself to yourself. Negative self-talk, if not addressed, can lead to actions that you may later regret. This could include missing opportunities, breaking relationships or missing valuable feedback. While it's natural to default to the negative, making concerted efforts to shift your focus to positive self-talk will lead to reduced negative physical, mental and emotional impacts.

Positive self-talk will lead to more success. It will also spark your confidence to speak up, to ask for what you want and to go for opportunities others might not feel courageous enough to go for, even when it feels awkward, uncomfortable or risky to do so. Importantly, positive self-talk will give you courage. Remember that courage is not about the absence of fear. It's acting despite the presence of fear!

As a leader your voice matters and your interpersonal communication skills matter. The people you lead want to hear from you, whether that's to receive direction, a decision or an endorsement. They rely on your input to know what's going on. And they look to you for your ideas for improving processes, problem solving and seizing opportunities.

Clear, concise and correct are given expectations when communicating but what others really want are connection, character, curiosity and calm. These traits help people feel safe. And safe employees will be loyal and productive employees. So, continuously improving your interpersonal communication skills is an investment that bears exponential returns.

With positive self-talk and exceptional interpersonal communication skills, you'll have the confidence and courage to speak up. You'll find it easier to be influential in those moments when it matters.

Add in your exceptional self-awareness and emotional intelligence and you'll also have the discernment to know when not to speak up or to let the situation be because interference will only make the situation worse.

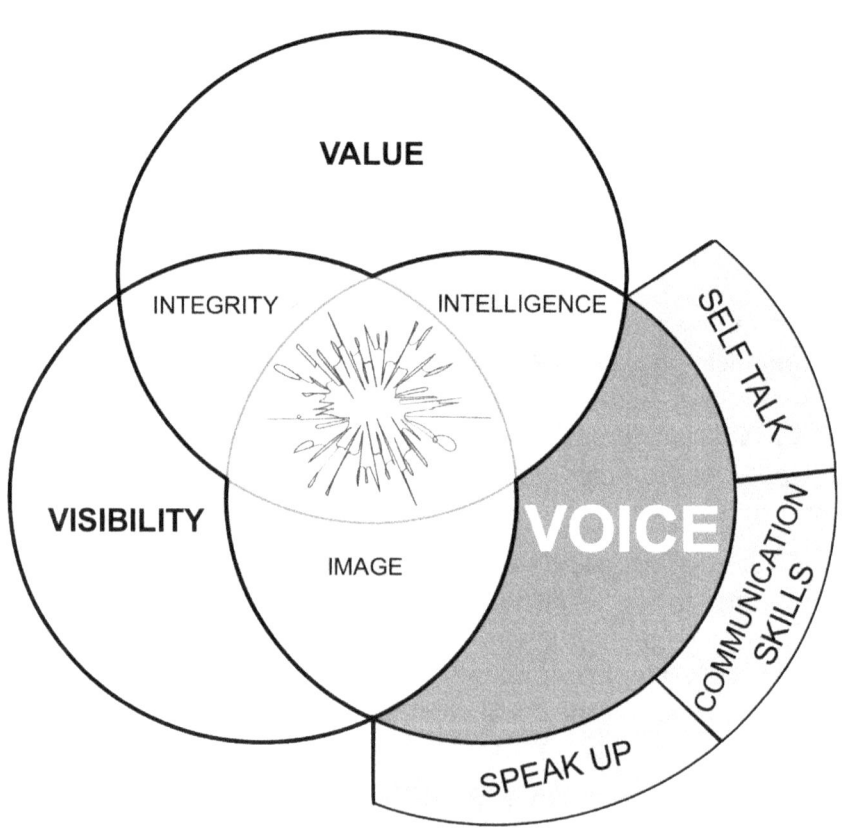

You can't find your voice if you don't use it.
—Austin Kleon

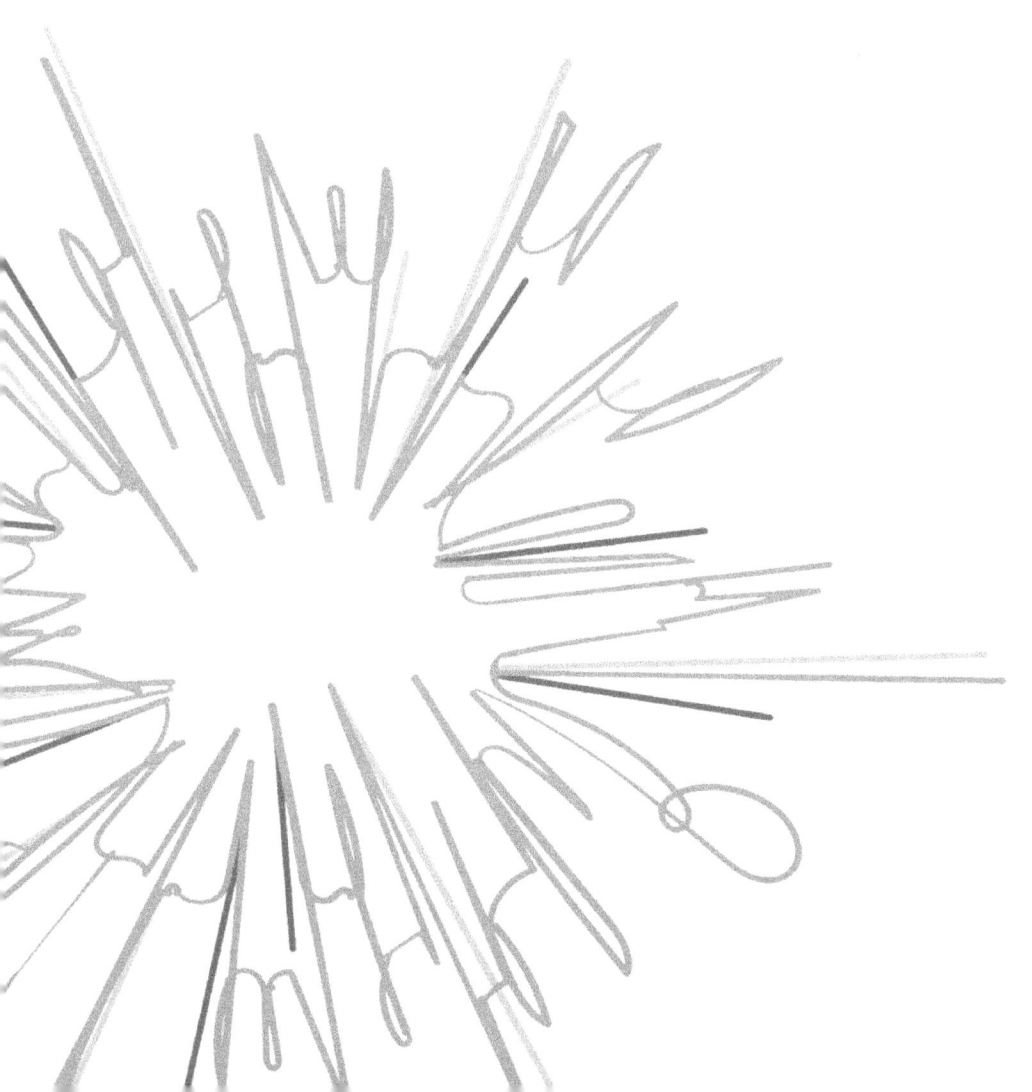

What can your voice do to influence?

Working on your voice (to match your profile) can help break any unconscious bias that might be at the table.

Stop listening to your voice! Start feeling your voice.

Lisa Lockland-Bell
Voice Coach

Snap to watch the full interview.

> What I appreciate about Lisa's statement about feeling your voice is her invitation to connect with your voice at a level deeper than just auditory. Have you noticed you 'sound' different when you hear your voice on a recording? This reminds me that how I hear my voice when speaking, versus when recorded, and versus when others hear my voice will vary. Therefore, it's important to focus on how I want my voice to portray who I am, more than just a sound, and how I want my voice to reinforce my confidence and influence as a leader.
>
> You can spark your self-leadership by strengthening your connection to your voice. Paying attention to how you say what you say as well as the message you intend.

Five Voice Tips to Sound Credible, Professional and Confident

In a Yale University study of voice-only communication, psychologist Michael W. Kraus[16] conducted five experiments to determine that voice-only communication – our tone, pitch, volume – may be the primary source of revealing our emotions.

1. Vocal First Impression

Know that you have a vocal first impression. When speaking, it happens in the first half second! That's how long it takes for someone to judge how trustworthy you are.

One of the most prominent places where you give a vocal first impression is on the phone or in a camera off online meeting. Your hello matters, make it a happy hello. Keep in mind that people can hear your mood in your voice.

2. Go for low but not rock bottom

Think of the famous voices you like to hear, do you like James Earl Jones, Morgan Freeman, Sam Elliott, Meryl Streep, Mila Kunis, Cate Blanchett? What is it about their voice you like?

Proper breathing helps soften and create a more pleasant sounding voice. Diaphragmatic breathing is the key to sounding softer and yet more powerful. To breath diaphragmatically is to take slow deep breaths, contracting the diaphragm (pulling it down with the in-breath).

I was once called onto stage to present on a topic I had not prepared for and about 15 minutes earlier than my scheduled keynote speech. It threw me and I forgot to breath properly. The first few moments on stage felt like hell: I know I sounded like I was totally out of breath and my voice was stuck in a higher pitch than more normal range. It was probably only moments but it seemed like an eternity to

---

16 https://www.apa.org/pubs/journals/releases/amp-amp0000147.pdf

breathe deeply, slow it down, re-engage my normal (lower) voice range and regain my own confidence.

Think of how you sound in different situations; for example, compare how your voice sounds when talking to someone really important such as a boss compared to how you might sound with your best friends. The voice that is the relaxed on is most likely the one you use with your friends, as it's the calm, engaged and relaxed one. This is the one that will sound more confident and credible.

3. Slow down

When you speak quickly you risk adding a sense of urgency and therefore adding pressure onto the shoulders of your audience. The people who are listening to you will feel uncomfortable. Check the pace of your voice, not everything is urgent, aim for your voice to engage and invite.

4. Record yourself

Listening to your recorded voice will help you pick up on pitch, tone, pace and volume. You'll also hear any filler words, like um, okay, so, ah. You will be able to also hear if you waffle on or need to expand on your message.

It's not always easy to listen to yourself, lots of people don't like hearing a recording of themselves, yet it's a truly valuable exercise you can do to get immediate feedback.

5. Smile

As long as it's not a serious matter where smiling is inappropriate, remind yourself to smile when you speak. Smiling helps your tone to be more friendly and warm.

Does your voice support your profile?
—Lisa Lockland-Bell, Voice Coach

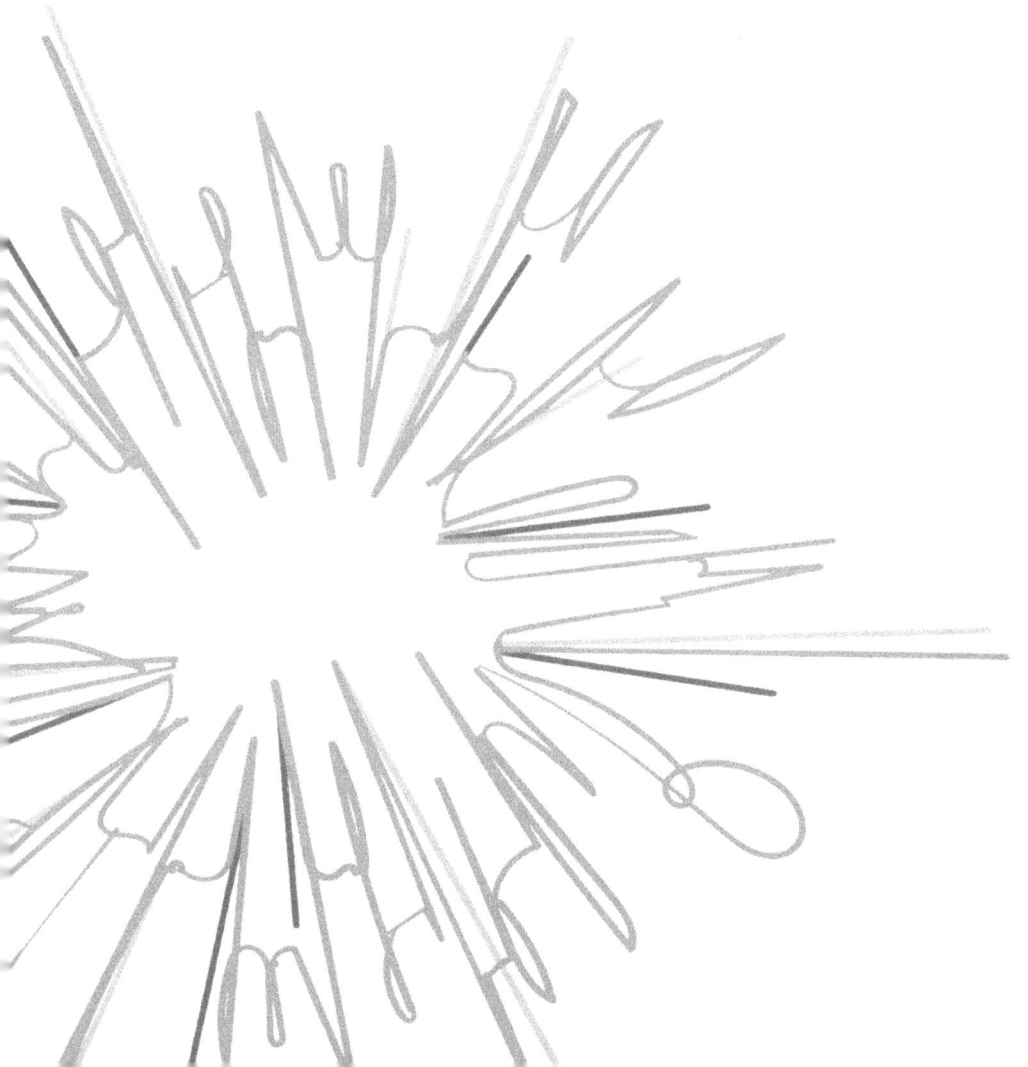

CHAPTER NINE

SELF-TALK:
IT'S NO ONE ELSE'S JOB TO LIKE YOU!

STRATEGY FOUR

Your self-talk is the script that frames your life. As Wright Thurston, a CEO and leadership expert, says, 'Self-talk is the most powerful form of communication because it either empowers you or it defeats you'.

According to *Healthline*[17], the benefits of self-talk include:

- increased vitality
- greater life satisfaction
- improved immune function
- reduced pain
- better cardiovascular health
- better physical well-being
- reduced risk of death
- less stress and distress

As a leader, your self-talk will help or hinder your:

- decision-making quality and speed
- feedback conversations

---

17 Holland, Kimberley. 'Positive Self-Talk: How Talking to Yourself Is a Good Thing'. *Healthline*. June 26, 2020. Accessed at https://www.healthline.com/health/positive-self-talk.

- preparedness to delegate
- clarity in setting boundaries and expectations
- self-care
- self-empathy
- self-mastery
- motivation
- preparedness for challenges and opportunities
- career progression

Interestingly, an article published by the *National Science Foundation* summarised a study that found, 'Of those thousands of thoughts, 80% were negative, and 95% were exactly the same repetitive thoughts as the day before'.[18]

Without actively identifying and working on any negative self-talk there can be significant consequences[19], such as:

- Feeling worthless, inferior or hopeless
- Anxiety, panic or shyness
- Feeling angry and frustrated
- Feelings of shame or guilt
- Depression

Types of Self-Talk

Negative self-talk is also referred to as cognitive distortion or distorted thinking. It's obvious that negative distorted thinking or

---

[18] Antanaityte, Neringa. 'Mind Matters: How To Effortlessly Have More Positive Thoughts'. TLEX Institute. Accessed at https://tlexinstitute.com/how-to-effortlessly-have-more-positive-thoughts/.

[19] If you are experiencing any of these please seek out professional advice from your health care provider.

negative self-talk can trigger the destructive consequences listed, but so too can distorted positive thinking. Some examples include[20]:

Labelling: This is where you label yourself and it's a form of overgeneralisation about yourself.

> *Negative Distortion:* Thinking of yourself as a loser because you made a small mistake and therefore you put less effort in going forward.
>
> *Positive Distortion:* Thinking of yourself as a winner can motivate but the reality is as humans we will win, lose and break even.

Assumptions: This is where you try to be a mind reader about how other people think and feel.

> *Negative Distortion:* Assuming that everyone else finds life easy. For example, attending networking events may be a challenge for you but as you look around the room you assume everyone finds it easy and enjoyable.
>
> *Positive Distortion:* Thinking that a team member likes, respects or even adores you when they may actually be very frustrated, disengaged or annoyed with you.

All or Nothing: This is where you think in black and white, all or nothing. There are no in-betweens or shades of grey.

> *Negative Distortion*: Thinking that one failure means you're a total failure.
>
> *Positive Distortion*: Thinking you're superior when you have a single win.

---

[20] There are many more examples worth exploring. I recommend you check out: https://feelinggood.com/2014/01/06/secrets-of-self-esteem-2-negative-and-positive-distortions/.

'You idiot, Sally!'

This was one my most common self-talk phrases when I made mistakes. I sometimes even said it out loud. While I thought of this as merely a throw-away line, it had become a strong and ingrained destructive phrase. The more I said it the more it became part of me.

Then one day, just after I had berated myself aloud for a mistake I had made, a dear friend questioned me. She said, 'If I made that mistake would you say that me? Would you say, 'You idiot?'

'Of course not!', I replied somewhat upset that she'd think I'd think that of her. She went on. 'I'd never say that to you either, but I notice you say it a lot to yourself when you make a mistake, even ridiculous tiny mistakes. I'd prefer it if you didn't speak to my friend like that.'

What an amazing gift to receive. Her words helped me to see the negative impact my self-talk was having on myself and even on others.

Of course, positive self-talk is not about lying to yourself. It's not about putting a positive spin on everything that happens no matter what. In fact, true positive self-talk is realistic, confident and specific. For example:

False positive self-talk:

> *I'm happy in this role. I only apply for promotions because it's the done thing around here.*

True positive self-talk:

> *I want a promotion, so I know I need to focus on developing the right skills in readiness for the role.*

or

> *I really like being at this level. I feel I can make an impact here and I don't want a more senior role as I will not have the access to the people and work I enjoy.*

Do you hear your self-talk? Hearing your self-talk is the first step to improving it. To really listen to how you speak to yourself, take a few days to monitor and track your self-talk. Over that period, simply mark when your self-talk is positive or negative, and track key words you use repeatedly.

Some examples of negative self-talk may include:

- It's too complicated.
- I don't have the resources.
- There's no way I can do that.
- I've never done it before.
- I look terrible today.
- I'm always getting it wrong.
- I'm stupid.
- I'm a failure.
- I can't seem to get organised.

- It's going to be another one of those days.
- If only I had more time.
- I never catch a break.

As you read through the list, notice that these are not facts. They are opinions or subjective. Furthermore, they are statements without a solution or framework for progress or moving forward. They basically suggest to give up.

Practice: Understanding Your Self-Talk

What is your self-talk? What statements do you hear yourself say often? Write them below.

_____

_____

_____

_____

_____

_____

As you start noticing your self-talk pay attention to what is happening in that same moment. What triggered the self-talk?

Self-Talk	Trigger

If you are not sure of the triggers to negative self-talk, reflect on these questions:

1. Think of a project you have wanted to start but didn't. What did you do or say to yourself about why you haven't started?

   _____
   _____

2. Think of a very busy, overwhelming and stressful day. What were you saying to yourself throughout the course of the day?

   _____
   _____

3. Recall the last time someone paid you a compliment. What did you say to yourself at the time the person gave you the compliment?

   _____
   _____

4. Recall a time when you were given some feedback or were criticised by someone whose opinion you valued. What did you tell yourself at the time of that incident?

   _____
   _____

After looking at your self-talk analyse the impact and reword them into more constructive, true, positive self-talk. By way of example, let's take my 'You idiot, Sally!' self-talk. The constructive true, positive alternative is:

> *That way didn't quite go to plan. That's a lesson for me for next time.*

Rephrasing negative and destructive self-talk into positive and constructive self-talk, and identifying the triggers that brought on that negative self-talk in the first instance, will help you be better equipped to make more positive, helpful and constructive choices when challenges come your way. You will think clearer and more calmly and be able to find solutions more quickly.

Negative self-talk	Rephrased into positive self-talk

Bye-Bye Bob!

Social Worker and author Melody Wilding suggests naming your inner critic. Rather than saying you are talking negatively about yourself, separate the self-talk by creating psychological distance through personalising it. You might call that inner critic The Joker, Darth Vader, Voldemort or even Bob... anything that separates you from your thoughts.

What this process does is help increase cognitive defusion. Cognitive defusion is the process of looking *at* your thoughts rather than *from* them. When you practice cognitive defusion you are able to notice thoughts rather than instinctively buying into the thought. You are able to let the thoughts come and go rather than holding onto them.

With cognitive defusion you are also able to see thoughts for what they are, not for what they say they are. And you are able to recognise that your thoughts aren't always true, accurate or complete and certainly don't need to define who you are. You can also begin to see that negative or false thoughts simply don't serve you well.

The result of this will be reduced stress and negativity, more regulated emotions and greater clarity of thinking—all elements that contribute to better self-leadership.

An executive client of mine, Jason, decided to call his negative self-talk, Bob. Whenever Bob popped in to give his two cents worth of destructive negative self-talk, Jason would say, *'Oh hi Bob. I'm a bit busy right now. I'm working on XYZ and I'm excited as it's a challenge and I'm learning new things as I go. Would you mind keeping it down?'*

Jason did share that he, at times, tells Bob where to go in no uncertain terms. He admitted that felt pretty cathartic!

When Jason and I would meet we'd have a bit of a laugh about the conversations he and Bob would have. But it was clear that these inner conversations contributed to putting the negative self-talk into perspective and minimising its impact. Furthermore, Jason said that over time the negative self-talk began to fade more quickly than before. He felt that talking to Bob separated Jason's abilities from the negative self-talk leaving him feeling more confident and being more productive.

Practice: Claim Your Inner Conversations

Give your inner critic a name:

_____

_____

_____

_____

Next time your self-talk turns to the negative, speak to that self-talk as that character. You may want to thank the character for pointing out some things you hadn't thought of but also invite the character to allow you to get on with your work.

What did you wish you knew about self-leadership before you stepped into your first leadership role?

I wish I'd known how hard it was and how seriously you have to focus, not on being a leader, because that's the external perception, but on living as a leader, which comes from within, and it's that inner core.

It had never occurred to me that it wasn't about what I did or even about what I said, it was about who I was. And so the question that I wish I had learned to ask earlier was who am I being right now? And who do I truly want to be, to be effective right now?

Julie Garland McLellan
CEO, The Director's Dilemma

Snap to watch the full interview.

Living as a leader starts from within! Julie sums up self-leadership beautifully in this quote.

You can spark your self-leadership by reflecting on the questions Julie poses:

Who are you being right now?

Who do I truly want to be to be effective right now?

CHAPTER TEN

INTERPERSONAL COMMUNICATION SKILLS: THE REAL CONNECTOR FOR PERSONAL AND PROFESSIONAL SUCCESS!

STRATEGY FIVE

While self-leadership is predominantly an inside job—being the process and ability to lead one's self—almost everything you do will impact others. You simply don't go through this world without communicating with others.

Interpersonal communication is the process of sending and receiving information between two or more people. Having effective interpersonal communication skills means that the people you are interacting with will understand your message and intent and will positively relate with you. And of course, having success at taming the negative self-talk influences your communication with others.

Without good quality communication skills, you can land yourself in all manner of trouble. Misunderstandings, broken relationships, conflict, costly mistakes, career impediments and even job loss—all are possible if your communication is not clear and correct. Survey after survey ranks communication as a high priority with many ranking communication skills in the top five essential leadership skills. For example, social media platform LinkedIn published an article in 2016 discussing a survey they conducted that revealed communication as the most in-demand soft skill[21].

The University of Phoenix Research Institute, in their publication *Future Work Skills 2020*[22] listed ten skills for the future workforce. Of the ten, more than half are directly linked to communication skills.

10 Future Work Skills

1. Sense-making: The ability to determine the deeper meaning or significance of what is being expressed.
2. Social intelligence: The ability to connect to others in a deep and direct way, and to sense and stimulate reactions and desired interactions.
3. Cross-cultural competency: The ability to operate in different cultural settings.
4. Computational thinking: The ability to translate vast amounts of data in abstract concepts and to understand data-based reasoning.
5. New media literacy: The ability to critically assess and develop content that uses new media forms, and to leverage these media for persuasive communication.
6. Transdisciplinarity: Literacy in and an ability to understand concepts across multiple disciplines.
7. Cognitive load management: The ability to discriminate and filter information for importance, and to understand how to maximise cognitive functioning using a variety of tools and techniques.
8. Virtual collaboration: The ability to work productively, drive engagement and demonstrate presence as a member of a virtual team.

---

21 Berger, Guy. 'Data Reveals The Most In-Demand Soft Skills Among Candidates'. *LinkedIn*. August 30, 2016. Accessed at https://www.linkedin.com/business/talent/blog/talent-strategy/most-indemand-soft-skills.

22 Institute for the Future for the University of Phoenix Research Institute. 'Future Work Skills 2020'. Retrieved from https://www.iftf.org/uploads/media/SR-1382A_UPRI_future_work_skills_sm.pdf.

Improving these skills positively impacts how you communicate and lead others. Improving these skills will give you stronger self-leadership and the belief in yourself to handle the challenges the future will bring.

Three Filters In Your Interpersonal Communication

Neurolinguistic programming (NLP), developed by Richard Bandler and John Grinder, is a model of communicating. It focuses in particular on how we receive, process and then act on information from the outside world. According to NLP there are three perceptual filters which affect the quality of our communications. These are distortion, deletion and generalisation.

Distortion

Distortion is the shifting or modifying of the interpretation of information, or misrepresenting information, as a way of making sense of or influencing our own self-image. In an article by Mark I. Johnson and Matt Hudson in the *Journal of Pain Management*, the authors stated that distortion helps to confirm pre-existing beliefs so they are linked with cognitive biases[23]. In other words, distortion can reaffirm the negative self-talk we already have, and help solidify it further in our minds. A distorted self-image doesn't just impact self-talk it also affects interpersonal communication.

Deletion

Deletion is the filtering and omitting of information. Given the vast amount of information we are exposed to continuously throughout our every waking minute, it can seem like a relief to delete even a bit of information so we can manoeuvre our way through life a little more easily. However, deleting or ignoring some information

---

[23] Johnson, Mark I. and Hudson, Matt. 'Generalizing, deleting and distorting information about the experience and communication of chronic pain'. *Future Medicine*. 1 August 2016. Accessed at https://www.futuremedicine.com/doi/10.2217/pmt-2016-0028.

because it's deemed meaningless, when it isn't meaningless to others or to a given situation, can have a significantly negative impact.

Generalising

Generalising is the averaging of information, such as applying one experience to a collection of experiences. While generalisations can be helpful as a foundation to further learning and understanding (as opposed to a stereotyping), they can also be harmful. Sometimes they can include or imply something incorrectly or lead to excluding what could be valuable opportunities. Generalisations tend to show up as broad-brush statements. For example, *all* the reports are a waste of time. Or the boss is *never* on time.

The key to self-leadership and successful interpersonal communication is to know that everyone can be at the mercy of these filters of distortion, deletion and generalisation. Stress, overwhelm, juggling multiple priorities, dealing with difficult employees and looming deadlines can all trigger a filter. So it's essential to check and clarify understanding of a message or information through questioning.

> *What part of this information is being ignored?*
> *Why might this be so?*
> *What part of this information is being changed to fit this situation?*
> *Why might this be so? For what benefit?*
> *Is this a generalisation, and if so, does this help us learn and develop or will this hinder future opportunities or cause some other form of harm?*

Practice: Distortion, Deletion, Generalisation

During the next team meeting pay attention to how you're listening to the information being shared and ask yourself if you're distorting or deleting anything.

What was the topic?

_____
_____
_____
_____

What part of this information is being ignored?

_____
_____
_____
_____

Why are you ignoring this information?

_____
_____
_____
_____

What part of this information is being changed to fit this situation?

_____
_____
_____
_____

Why might this be so, for what benefit?

_____
_____
_____
_____

At any time during the meeting did you notice yourself, or anyone else, applying any generalisations? If so, what were they?

_____
_____
_____
_____

Being able to identify when you may use these filters means you can then adjust your listening, thinking and subsequent communicating.

Practice: Assess your Communication

This assessment is designed to explore any potential you may have for being a source of miscommunication or other communication mistakes. The more honest your answers are, the better you will be placed to improve your interpersonal communication skills.

Use this scale to score your behaviour:

5 – I constantly do this
4 – I frequently do this
3 – I occasionally do this
2 – I infrequently do this
1 – I do not do this at all

___ 1. I think before I speak because I'm aware that my words may not mean the same thing to me as they might for other people.

___ 2. Before communicating, verbally or nonverbally, I fully understand who my receiver is and how my message may affect their perception of my message.

___ 3. When communicating with my friends, I'm honest and open about what I'm sharing.

___ 4. While I'm communicating, I'm looking for signs that my message is being perceived just as I intend.

___ 5. I make sure I avoid using slang words and idioms with people who may be offended by them.

___ 6. When others are communicating with me, I understand that sometimes the message being sent may not be the same one I am perceiving or receiving.

___ 7. I ensure my messages are accurate and to the point.

___ 8. I do not use jargon with people who may not understand it.

___ 9. I explore ways to enhance my listening skills.

___ 10. I try to avoid using words that might trigger distress or confuse the receiver.

___ 11. I carefully choose the best medium for my message and the receiver: direct message, video call, email, face-to-face meeting or telephone call.

___ 12. I work hard to listen to ideas I don't agree with.

____ 13. I devise opinions about what others say to me based on what I hear them say rather than what I think of them as a person.

____ 14. I know that the way I say something is just as important as what I say.

____ 15. I ensure my nonverbal communications match the meaning of what I want to convey to others.

_____ **Total Score**

What the results mean:

75 – 65	You are an exceptionally effective communicator who almost never causes misunderstandings.
55 – 64	You are an effective communicator who only occasionally causes communication failure.
45 – 54	You are an above average communicator with intermittent gaps. You cause some misunderstandings but less than your share.
35 – 44	Most people fall into this category. While things could be worse, there is room for improvement in your communication.
25 – 34	You may find that you're a frequent source of communication difficulties.
15 – 24	Your honesty is admirable, but it will take more than honesty to improve your communication effectiveness.

Reflect over your individual answers to the quiz questions. Note the three questions where you did not score so well. What can you do to improve that aspect of your communication?

_____

_____

_____

_____

_____

_____

SPARK Better Interpersonal Communication Skills

Listen More

Listening, real deep listening, can be exhausting. Yet, it can save time, money and relationships when we actively listen more deeply.

Author of *Deep Listening: Impact Beyond Words*, Oscar Trimboli, says, 'Listening is complex and nuanced. It's situational as well as relational. It's not just about what you hear. It's not just about what you see. It's much more than that. It's about respect'.

With active listening, you use all your sensory skills, including sight, sound, gestures and facial expressions, to enhance the communication process. This is what it means to listen with your whole body. You will retain more of what you have heard. Even better, you will be well placed to pick up on underlying feelings and ideas, allowing you to get to the heart of what the speaker is trying to convey.

Possibly the most difficult communication skill to learn, effective and productive listening requires hard work and participation. Active, attentive listening involves all your physical, emotional and intellectual faculties. To be a successful listener, you must accept the following ideas:

> **Accept that listening is as powerful as speaking.** What someone says to you is just as critical as what you have to say to them.
>
> **Appreciate listening saves time and effort.** When you listen you avoid many mistakes, misunderstandings and false starts.
>
> **Listening to everybody is important and worthwhile.** You can learn from each and every person you meet.

Listening is the precious gift that helps build relationships, solve problems, ensure understanding, resolve conflicts and improve accuracy.

Practice: Listening

Recall the last time you were in a conversation, and you knew the other person wasn't really listening to you. What thoughts and feelings come to mind about that experience? Write them below.

_____
_____
_____

The way you felt is worth keeping in mind the next time your mind wanders away from listening to others.

Check Understanding

A read receipt on an email is not the same as ensuring the message sent was understood as you intended. Sometimes simply saying, 'Did you understand that?' may not be enough. Checking to see if the message sent was the message received prevents many potentially costly and frustrating communication problems.

It's better to ask a brief set of questions to confirm that the message was understood accurately than to assume otherwise. As the message sender, if you ask clarifying and confirming questions, you can then hear the answers to those questions, and are best placed to make any necessary clarifications and communication adjustments before any costly errors or actions are taken.

Practice: Check Understanding

Think about the last time someone misunderstood you. What was the message about? What did you want the message receiver to do, think or say?

_____
_____
_____

Thinking about how they misunderstood you. What two questions could you have asked that would have helped check the understanding and eliminated the misunderstanding?

1. _____
2. _____

The message receiver can also help confirm the understanding by repeating the message back to the sender in their own words. For example, the receiver could say, 'Here's what I understand so far….'.

Think about the last time you misunderstood someone but didn't speak up. Consider using the following as a means of ensuring understanding:

> 'Thanks for this information. So that you and I know we are on the same page, this is what I understand you want from me… Is this correct?'

Use the Right Medium for the Message and the Receiver

Shooting off a quick email feels efficient and helps get 'one more thing' off your to-do list. Sending an email can also be a convenient way to avoid certain inevitable conversations. However, this can be a false convenience. The reality is it can backfire, and it often does.

An email lacks the depth and dimension that a phone call, video call or face-to-face conversation can provide. An email is not a two-way fluid conversation but rather a series of one-way monologues. And this can lead to communication confusion and frustration, and wasted time.

To reduce having to go back and forth—also known as email ping-pong—checking clarity and confirming actions and agreements, aim to use the platform or communication medium that makes the most of your body language, eye contact, tone and words and provides the opportunity for a two-way conversation. Of course, face-to-face is generally best but that's not going to be possible all the time.

Before communicating with anyone, slow down for just a moment and think clearly about how you can communicate the most effectively the first time. A great self-leader will take the time to ensure they are matching the medium to the message accurately.

The more complex the content of your message, the more likely there will be questions or points requiring extra clarification. In those cases, email is not going to be the best option. Email is, however, a critical business tool, and is often very useful. Once a conversation has occurred, an email can be used as a summary of the conversation, informing others of decisions, giving approvals and transferring relevant documents.

Say What You Mean

Sarah, a team leader, would send emails to her direct reports that would start with the line, *'Just a few changes...'*. However, the email would go on and on, mouse scroll after mouse scroll. There was rarely anything 'few' about any of Sarah's emails. When Sarah was made aware of the contradiction, she immediately adjusted her opening line.

Make your expectations clear

Sarah went a step further, however. She began to work more closely with her team to address the deeper communication issues she was having with her direct reports. As a result of that work she made some changes to her communication methods, including:

- As she was allocating work Sarah spent more time being clear in her expectations for how she expected the work to be completed, rather than waiting for something to be submitted and then having to re-work everything.
- Sarah would respectfully push back and ask for work to be resubmitted so that she didn't end up fixing other people's work.
- She also worked individually with team members to address specific task issues and help them meet her expectations.

Get to the Point

Period!

In Times of Uncertainty

In times of uncertainty employees want to hear from their leader, to know their leader has their back, is present and is open to ideas.

When employees don't hear from their leader, they will search for meaning, potentially get involved in gossip or make stuff up (not always intentionally in a bad way—but for an increased sense of safety and security). As a leader, in times of uncertainty, you may not have all the answers. But you can be present, listen, remind people to stay the current course and encourage team members to support each other. You can also help team members spark their own self-leadership through speaking up and sharing their ideas.

What did you wish you knew about self-leadership before you stepped into your first leadership role?

Understanding people better! We are ultimately people managers.

Karen Brown
Pharmacy Owner,
Terry White Chemmart, Arana Hills

Snap to watch the full interview.

This quote from Karen's interview links to the value of self-leadership for helping leaders to understand their people. Successful leaders focus on the people first so that the productivity follows.

You can spark yours and your team members self-leadership by asking questions, listening and learning about yourself and your people.

Raise your words not your voice—it is rain that grows flowers, not thunder.
—Rumi

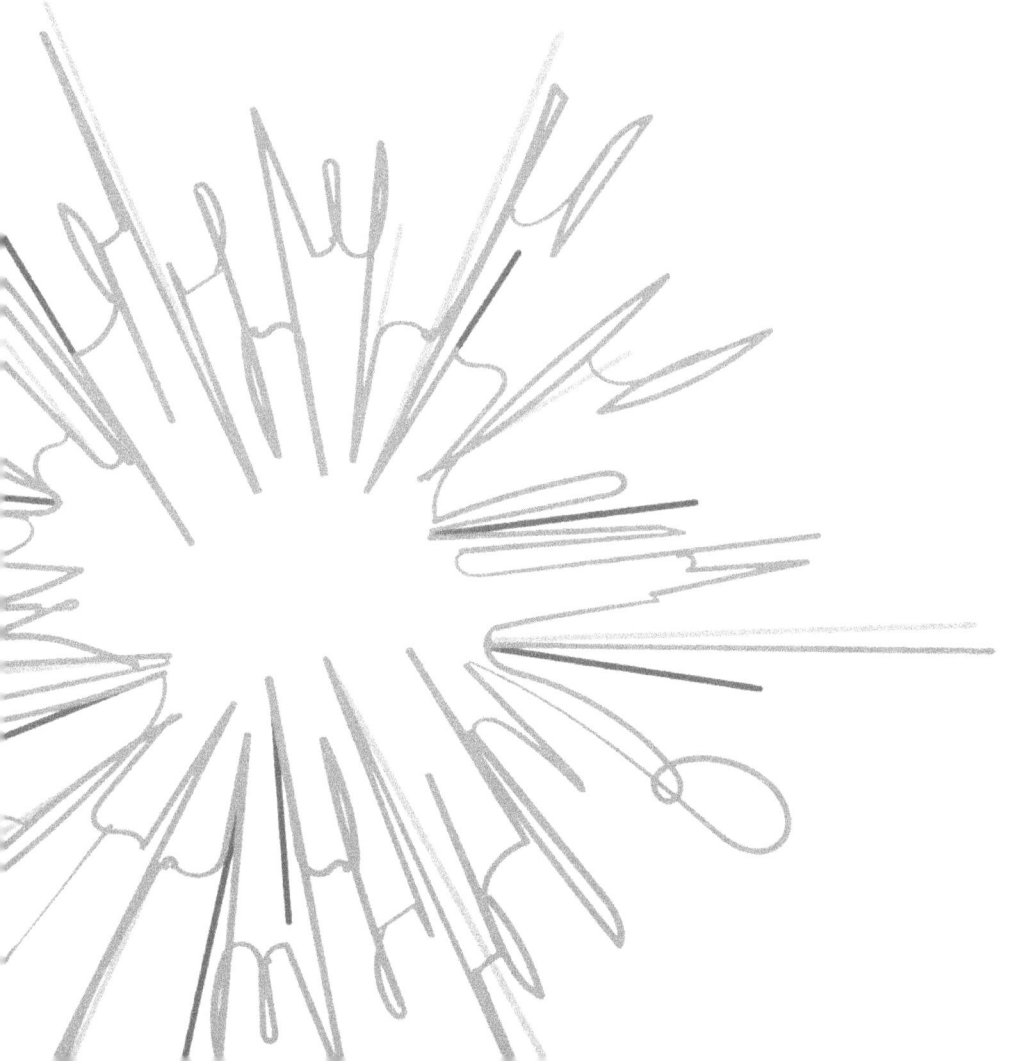

CHAPTER ELEVEN

SPEAK UP: WHO DOES YOUR SILENCE SERVE?

STRATEGY SIX

Marketing genius Seth Godin wrote:

When smart, committed people disagree about the answer to a question, you've found a question worth pursuing and a discussion worth having.

Remembering that there are often differing, contradicting views could actually help you keep calm and confident in the face of disagreement, rather than get triggered into the fear of rejection, regret or failure. In fact, it can help you to speak up in a confident and constructive manner.

When discussing an issue with smart and committed people—your people—reminding yourself that they are clever and invested could be the anchor you use to stop, breathe and give yourself the opportunity to listen, be curious and hear all views. This makes you a better-informed leader about the issue at hand as well as giving you more general insight into your people.

An alternative way of looking at it is—if they didn't care they probably wouldn't disagree, debate or argue. On the other hand, a lack of discussion might appear as agreement or seem peaceful but without further investigation it'd probably be a sign of people not feeling engaged, invested or valued. This is a red flag for productivity in the short term and turnover or presenteeism in the longer term.

Conflict is an enormous topic with many nuances. Some of these nuances are understanding what to say when and how to speak up with confidence when you disagree with:

- direct reports
- peers
- senior leaders
- clients/customers
- key stakeholders
- decisions
- results
- feedback

Each situation will present you with a different intensity of internal and external conflict based on the perceived power that's present. In other words, the relationship you have with the person on the other side of the disagreement, the actual issue at hand and your confidence with the issue, in yourself and in the relationship.

Speaking up is not always easy but consider the cost of not speaking up. In the novel *Rodham*, the author Curtis Sittenfeld blends non-fiction and fiction. She mixes real facts, anecdotes and analysis to portray a different, fictional path for Hilary Rodham Clinton. But for our purpose, I want to focus on a single line in the book that sums up the value of speaking up:

Sittenfeld says, *'Sometimes speaking your mind is expensive, which doesn't mean it's not worth it'.*

Five Tips to Fire Up Your Confidence to Speak Up in Conflict Situations

Tip 1. Autonomic Overrides

Our nervous system, a network that accounts for three percent of our body weight, works 24 hours a day, communicating at levels we barely understand. Within our nervous system there are two systems acting in balance with each other: the sympathetic nervous system (SNS) and the parasympathetic nervous system (PSNS). SNS is often called our 'fight or flight' system, while PSNS is responsible for our 'relaxation response'. Together these two systems regulate our breathing, heart rate, circulation, hormones and digestion. Unfortunately, these systems also tend to overreact to daily stress, such as we might feel when we're in conflict.

When we're in conflict too often, over time it creates an imbalance that leads to stress-related problems such as slow muscular recovery, injuries and irritability. As it is hard to turn off the stress response, we can override it by turning on the relaxation response. The relaxation response is stimulated when the respiratory system is even, smooth and relaxed.

Autonomic overrides are actions that can help trigger the PSNS and help us to stay calm, focused and in control rather than dip into fears of failure, regret or rejection or even fight or flight.[24]

Some of these include:

a. **Mindful breathing, stretching and moving.** These actions can help you stimulate the PSNS.
b. **Labelling.** Calling the situation what it is or putting a situation into context in a positive, helpful way can help you dip out of SNS and into PSNS. Take Seth Godin for example, who, when conflict arose in a meeting, labelled it by saying, *'This must be an important issue as we have contradictory responses. We have clever and committed people here. Let's discuss and listen to each other.'*

---
24 https://briandorfman.com/override-the-stress-response/

Tip 2.   Leverage before Lunging

Before briefing the boss on a sensitive or contentious issue that you know may trigger conflict, consider who you could speak with first. Who is a trusted advisor to the boss, maybe their executive assistant, an office manager, or another head of a department? Consulting with them may give you valuable advice on how to present your information, as well as support you in doing so.

Tip 3.   Observe Before Speaking Out

Before you begin an interaction with someone, take a moment to reflect on the person with whom you're about to engage. Think about the characteristics that you've observed in them in the past. That time you take in reflection will help you ensure you're calm. But more importantly, you can use that time to consider how you can adapt your style to what you've observed about the person, especially in real time conversations based on their reactions. The more you observe others, the more you can understand how they engage with others and the more confident you will be in handling the tough conversations.

Consider someone who triggers conflict or stress in you when you communicate with them:

- Does the person ask questions?
- Does this person often push back on ideas before they've been fully expressed?
- Does this person drive or push their ideas onto others?
- Is this person an intensive and active listener?
- Does this person have open or closed body language?
- Online, does this person avoid having their camera on?

When you take the time to learn about how that person communicates, this will help you adjust your communication style to suit the situation. It will also reduce judgements that can interfere with your leadership and communication.

Tip 4. Double Line Spacing

I was listening to a wonderful speaker and friend, Jessica Pettitt, give a keynote speech about judging and judgement. She made a profound comment that can positively impact self-leadership and communication. What Jess suggested is that all humans judge. It's what we do. And it's hard to stop. So when you judge, do so with double line spacing and extra wide margins so that you can edit your judgements as you learn more and connect deeper.

You can apply this to yourself and your difficult communications, too. When it comes time to work with others that you may not always agree with (and that's a good thing), remember to reserve space to change your mind, and your judgements. A good leader will always take on board new information to help them change and grow. A good communicator will as well.

Tip 5. Shadow and Light

Conflict often arises due to a values violation—for example, people are late, don't listen, interrupt or keep disrespecting your boundaries. If values violations are not dealt with they can fester and significantly damage relationships, the culture of the team or even the whole organisation.

Without being flippant you can help tame fears and spark confidence by turning the shadow into the light. In other words, rephrasing a values violation into a positive and helpful assertion. This can help you then approach the person with a more positive word choice and a calmness and confidence that will enable you to resolve the issue. Approaching another person this way, rather than from a place of frustration and aggression will give you the best chance for an amicable resolution where the other person will be more willing to adhere to your values.

For example,

> Value Violation (Shadow): *'I hate it when Mary is late.'*
>
> Value Reframe (Light): *I really appreciate it when Mary arrives on time for our meetings.'*
>
> Value Violation (Shadow): *'It really ticks me off when Ben takes the credit for the team's hard work.'*
>
> Value Reframe (Light): *'The team works hard and it's great when Ben acknowledges their effort.'*

Practice: Shadow to Light

What is one of your value violations? Write it below as a pet peeve, i.e., the shadow:

_____

_____

_____

_____

_____

_____

Now reframe that into a more positive, value reframe, i.e., the light:

_____

_____

_____

_____

_____

_____

Get Your Message Heard

1. **Understand what you want.**

   What are you actually asking for? Be clear about your goal.

2. **Understand who your audience is.**

   Be clear about who you are speaking to. Consider their pain points in relation to what you want. How is what you're asking for going to work for them? In other words, what's in it for them to say yes to you, to hear your view or to hear your perspective?

   Think about how they like to hear input. Express your needs in way that aligns with that preference.

3. **Plan and rehearse.**

   Mark Twain made famous (and Anglicised) the French mathematician and philosopher, Balise Pascal's quote, *'If I had more time, I would have written a shorter letter.'* Short, concise and precise communications are the best method for getting your message heard. But if you're not clear on your message then you will run the risk of waffling. This is very closely linked to knowing what you want, the goal of your message.

   There is a quick process you can use when time is short to consolidate your message and minimise the waffling. Simply answer the following questions in as few words as possible:

   - Subject – What will you tell them?
   - Purpose – Why do they need to know?
   - Outcome – What do you want them to do, say or feel?
   - Relevance – Why is this important?

   These questions help you to be informative without the overwhelm. With clarity in your message, you will avoid pointing out irrelevant issues, that can confuse the thrust of your point.

When you combine this with knowing your audience you will be able to create the right words for the right people. This will give you far more influence, and you will sound more credible because you will feel more confident.

As part of your planning, you will also want to consider how you will use your body to convey the right impression you want the audience to have about you and what you want. By way of example many leaders, especially women, will stand in front of a meeting with one leg crossed in front of the other. This gives the unfortunate impression that they may need the bathroom! Many leaders who present with one or both hands in their pockets run the risk of coming across as arrogant or giving the impression they wish they were elsewhere.

At the very least sit or stand up straight with your shoulders back but relaxed (not forced back). Work to breathe from your diaphragm rather than your chest or throat (let your stomach fill with air). These physical actions will help you look and feel more secure and confident while delivering your message.

4. Harness your nerves

I've never understood the old piece of advice that if you're nervous imagine your audience naked. How does that not make you more nervous or even feel creeped out? But it is important to work on harnessing your nerves. Because speaking up, especially when there are more senior leaders in the room can trigger a nervous reaction.

I've been a professional speaker for many years and people assume I don't get nervous. I do and I like it! Instead of finding ways to rid the nerves, I thank the nerves for giving me energy. I also find that if I'm not nervous I wonder if I'm being complacent at the speaking engagement. I harness the nervous energy into bringing the right energy to my audience.

Shift your mindset to harness the energy those nerves are surging in you. Turn that energy into enthusiasm and passion for your point or proposal. Remember that, despite their rank, everyone in that room is human and most people see public speaking as terrifying.

Most audiences want their speaker, you, to do well, to get their message across clearly and convincingly.

5. Options and Objections

Consider what objections might be put to you so that you have options and recommendations ready if your point or pitch is challenged. Don't let the excitement of your idea, and the potential that perhaps only you can see initially, blind you into not being grounded, calm and ready for others who might not agree with you.

By doing this work before you speak up, it also helps you minimise the risk of waffling. You'll feel prepared so you'll feel confident. And having these elements prepared also gives the impression of being confident and that helps you be more influential.

What did you wish you knew about self-leadership before you stepped into your first leadership role?

There's a difference between a fast decision and a good decision. Mindfulness. There's some aspect of that to self-leadership because it is taking those seconds and minutes, and just saying, where am I coming from? What am I basing that on, compared to, maybe, what I would like to be basing that on.

David Pace Ph.D.
Nuclear Energy Industry Research, USA.

Snap to watch the full interview.

David invites leaders to take a moment. In the fast paced, demanding world of work it's easy to be swept up in everyone's urgency which can then force fast decision making. Taking a mindful moment to check the reality of the urgency and then to ask what needs to be considered in order to make a good decision will always create the space for better outcomes for everyone.

You can spark your self-leadership by strengthening your mindfulness. Learn to pick up on the sense of urgency and the heightened energy that urgency triggers in yourself and others. Ask what the urgency is really about.

CHAPTER TWELVE

VISIBILITY: BEING SEEN AT THE RIGHT TIME FOR THE RIGHT REASON!

Out of sight equals out of mind and out of influence!

During a self-leadership workshop Jeremy, the head of a department, was sharing with me that he was frustrated that he was not getting opportunities to act in higher roles or take on bigger responsibilities. He felt overlooked and ignored. He also mentioned that he was often left off invites for meetings regarding work that he felt impacted him and his team.

Through exploring Jeremy's self-leadership via values, voice and visibility we discovered that Jeremy could do more to ensure he was being seen in the right places for the right reasons. In other words that he was getting a seat at the table! In short Jeremy needed to be more visible.

Jeremy is a hard worker who embraced early starts, late nights and often working weekends to ensure he and his team achieved and delivered their objectives. He didn't realise how keeping his head down and working hard kept him invisible. He was a firm believer that the results should speak for themselves when it comes to being seen and being recognised, acknowledged and rewarded. Unfortunately for Jeremy, he was most certainly out of sight, and therefore out of mind.

In Jeremy's case, he would often skip the townhall meetings, social functions and company events in favour of sneaking in some quiet time in the office to get ahead in his work. He was even more elusive by being quite inconsistent with attending the online meetings choosing to be on camera with his own team but not always on camera when meeting with the management team and senior leadership team meetings.

Sadly, just as in Jeremy's case, your great work is not always going to speak (loud enough) for itself. If you are not seen you will most likely not be front of mind for those who can allocate to you great opportunities, more resources or even promotions. But there are steps you can take to remedy this.

Mentoring can help make you more visible within and across an organisation or industry. I asked Jeremy about his mentoring experience. He had once had a mentor allocated to him in his early days as a frontline leader but hadn't really understood what mentoring was about and his mentor rarely connected with him. This has since made him a bit hesitant to look for other mentors as he felt that there was a big deal made of that mentoring opportunity only to have it fizzle to nothing. I knew that this could be an important part of Jeremy's self-leadership action plan.

Once we'd finished our analysis we worked together to set out Jeremy's self-leadership action plan. It included five key actions:

1. Always have the camera on when attending all online meetings.
2. Attend as many as possible company-wide events.
3. Meet with one colleague and one senior leader each fortnight to learn more about their role and strengthen his network and relationships.
4. Reach out to his people and culture department to learn about the mentoring program and explore how he can get involved again.
5. Identify people he admires who might be open to being his mentor.

Within seven months of working this plan, Jeremy had started being invited to more strategic meetings and key events. He'd also started a mentoring program and felt that he now had more influence with his boss. His immediate actions helped him feel more in charge of his career which made him feel more visible and therefore more confident. Following up with Jeremy he shared:

> *'I thought putting my head down and hard work was all that was needed but the harder I worked the less ahead I felt I was getting. From the learning at the self-leadership workshop, working my action plan, to focusing on being more visible to the senior leaders and other key influencers and decision makers, I then had opportunities to share ideas. I even got to do the 'humble brag' about the team, which, let's face it, reflected well on me. I can't complain about that! I've learned that I need to be seen in order to be far more influential. I'm glad I learned this now otherwise I would have just kept getting more and more upset with everyone else progressing past me without realising it was me who had to take action. I am a more engaged leader, my team are all doing well and I'm so much calmer and more confident.'*

Standing Out

Your self-image will be one driver for how you will show up in your workplace. A negative self-image will lead you to playing small. A positive self-image doesn't guarantee a win but it puts you in the game and shows others you're ready and willing to step up and stand out. Therefore, this third focus area of visibility, like the others, starts with the inner work, which in this case, is self-image. After all, how you see yourself will impact how you show up to others.

Your self-leadership development in this area also includes seeking out opportunities to be visible. Networking and mentoring will help you be visible in the right place with the right people. And the third area of visibility is to stand out. The key strategy to standing out starts with visualisation.

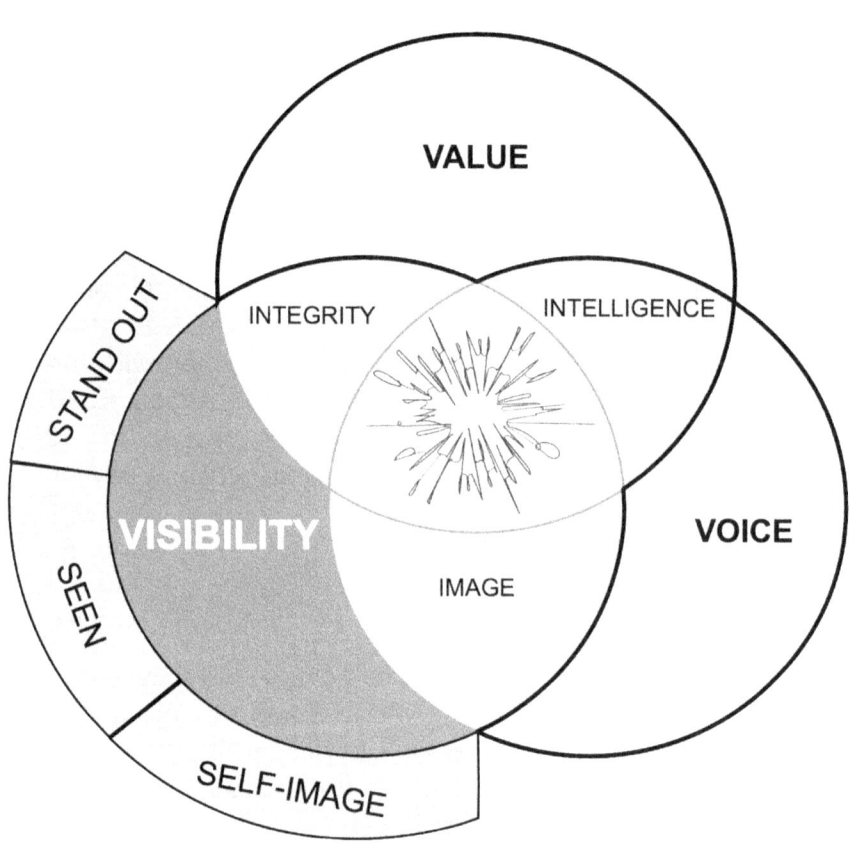

Remember, you have been criticizing
yourself for years and it hasn't worked.
Try approving of yourself and see what happens.
—Louise Hay

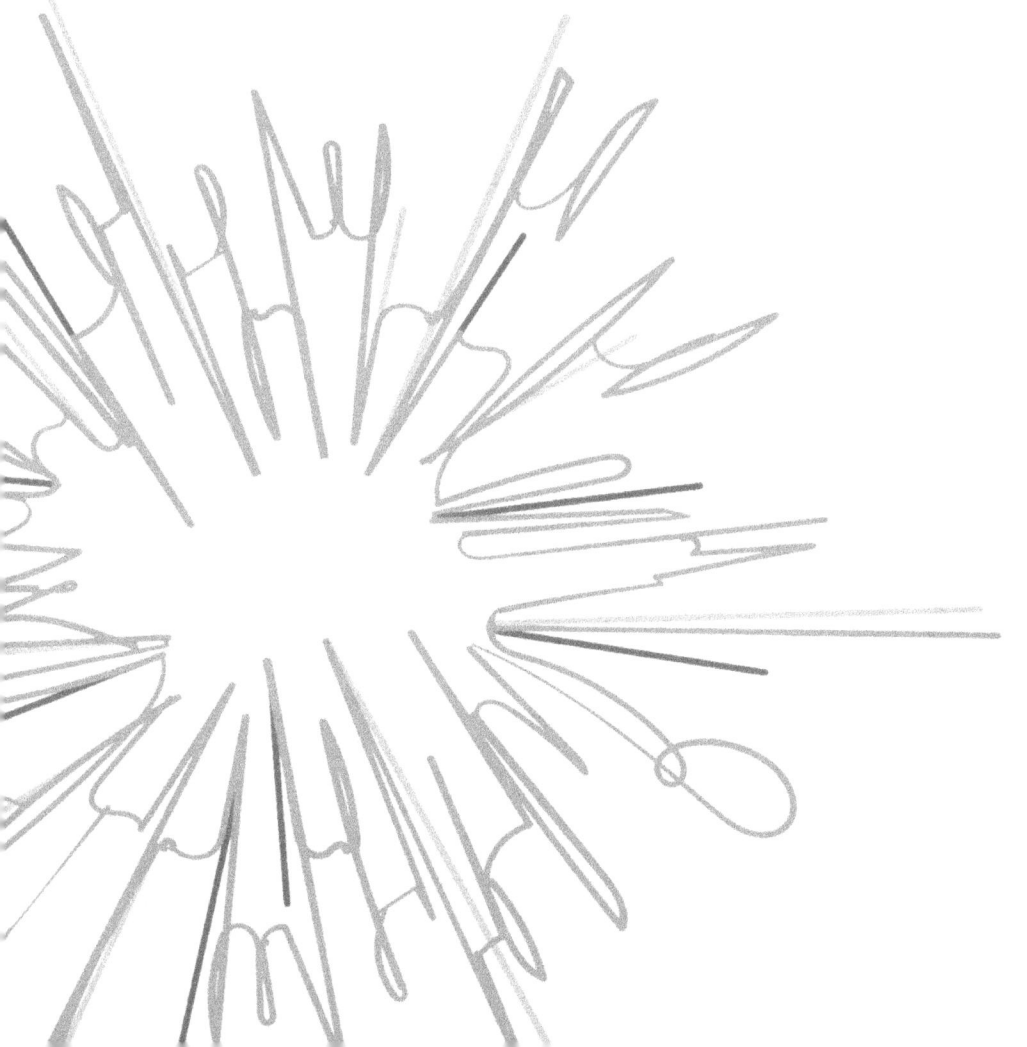

What did you wish you knew about self-leadership before you stepped into your first leadership role?

It goes back to my childhood, I wish I knew that I was bright.

Dr Karina Butera
Karina Butera Consulting

Snap to watch
the full interview.

> As a child we are influence by our surroundings. We are constantly receiving messages that inform who we are. However, as adults we have the power to control those surroundings and so control those messages.
>
> You can spark your self-leadership by strengthening your boundary setting; in reflections of those messages question and challenge how useful and accurate they are; and decide your own self-worth.

CHAPTER THIRTEEN

SELF-IMAGE: YOU DETERMINE YOUR WORTH!

STRATEGY SEVEN

Self-image is the personal views or mental images you have of yourself. If this collection of images are positive they will be your assets or strengths while those you see as negative will be weaknesses or liabilities.[25]

When getting to the bottom of your self-image, start with asking how do you define yourself? How do you define how you look? How do you define how smart, clever or intelligent you are? How do you define how well you're doing in your work and relationships?

A negative self-image could include:

- Seeing yourself as stupid or unintelligent.
- Seeing yourself as undesirable.
- When looking in the mirror you see an unhealthy, unattractive or unhappy person.
- You don't see yourself as being the ideal version of yourself.
- You believe others see these negative traits in you as well.

---

[25] If you feel you have a significant issue relating to your self-image, please do seek professional guidance, advice and support, such as the services a psychologist can provide.

A positive self-image could include:

- Seeing yourself as intelligent and smart.
- Seeing yourself as desirable.
- When looking in the mirror you see a happy, healthy and attractive person.
- You believe you are close to or working on being the ideal version of yourself.
- You think that others see these positive traits in you as well.

Self-image has many learned aspects. Your entire life has provided influences that have shaped your self-image, such as the experiences you've had with family, friends, teachers, bosses or relationships. However, you can choose which to embrace so they work for your benefit and ultimately lead to better self-leadership.

It's important that you control how you see yourself. Your self-image will affect how you feel which will then affect the way you interact with others and your environment. This poses an obvious link to confidence and influence and the decisions you make that affect your self-leadership as well as leading others.

Naturally, any negative self-image you have can lead you to over focus on faults, failures and imperfections, even distorting failure. On the other hand, a positive self-image is not about ignoring limitations but rather objectively identifying and accepting them as well as recognising your strengths and abilities.

As self-image is learned, this means it can be changed. It does not have to be fixed. Accepting yourself is a key starting point to a positive self-image. It is also influenced by being accepted and liked and loved by others, but it will most importantly start with you.

Practice: Spark your self-image

Identifying your strengths and learning to appreciate the good things in your life (gratitude practice) are two activities that can help you see yourself in a realistic and positive way.

Answer the following questions:

What are three to five life events, especially adverse events, that you have overcome?

1. _____
   _____
   _____

2. _____
   _____
   _____

3. _____
   _____
   _____

4. _____
   _____
   _____

5. _____
   _____
   _____

Who are the five to 10 people who have helped you to be the person you are today?

1. _____
2. _____
3. _____
4. _____
5. _____
6. _____
7. _____
8. _____
9. _____
10. _____

Who are the five to 10 people you've helped?

1. _____
2. _____
3. _____
4. _____
5. _____
6. _____
7. _____
8. _____
9. _____
10. _____

What are your top five life achievements?

1. _____
2. _____
3. _____
4. _____
5. _____

What are your top 10 skills?

1. _____
2. _____
3. _____
4. _____
5. _____
6. _____
7. _____
8. _____
9. _____
10. _____

What are the top 10 things you love about yourself?

1. _____
2. _____
3. _____
4. _____
5. _____

6. _____
7. _____
8. _____
9. _____
10. _____

Take some time to appreciate the things that you have benefitted from in your life. What are some of the good things that have happened to you? When you can appreciate these things, you will find gratitude easy, making your world view and self-image more positive.

Can you list 25 things you appreciate about your life?

1. _____
2. _____
3. _____
4. _____
5. _____
6. _____
7. _____
8. _____
9. _____
10. _____
11. _____
12. _____
13. _____
14. _____
15. _____
16. _____

17. _____
18. _____
19. _____
20. _____
21. _____
22. _____
23. _____
24. _____
25. _____

Can you add more? If so, keep listing all the things you appreciate in your life.

You can take it a step further and share your appreciation with those who might enjoy, value and, dare I say it, appreciate the appreciation!

_____
_____
_____
_____
_____
_____
_____
_____
_____

What did you wish you knew about self-leadership before you stepped into your first leadership role?

The leader looks like the person in your mirror.

Self-leadership is about reflection and understanding the power you wield over yourself and other people.

Victor Perton
Chief Optimism Officer

Snap to watch the full interview.

When you see yourself in the mirror do you see a leader?

Exceptional self-leadership takes reflection … check your reflection in the mirror.

CHAPTER FOURTEEN

SEEN: AN EAR, A HEART AND AN INSIGHT TO HELP YOU THINK AND SELF-LEAD!

STRATEGY EIGHT

'If I hadn't had mentors, I wouldn't be here today. I'm a product of great mentoring, great coaching… Coaches or mentors are very important.' PepsiCo CEO Indra Nooyi says as she credits mentoring for helping her break the glass ceiling – the social barrier to promotion – in business.

The Value of Mentorship

Firing up your self-leadership through the support and guidance of a mentor is invaluable. Mentors are able to sponsor you, so mentors within your organisation or industry can support and nurture your visibility.

The 44th President of the United States, Barack Obama, is the first to shine the spotlight on his early law career mentor, Michelle Robinson (aka Michelle Obama). It is their style to shine the light on others doing great work and he credits his wife as being the success and support behind his achievements.

Cricket sporting legend Sachin Tendulkar mentored Virender Sehwag to be the best version of himself, helping him to find his own batting style rather than trying to mimic or copy Tendulkar. Sehwag is widely regarded as one of the most destructive (in a sporting positive way) batsmen of all time.

Mentoring is a key activity that can, amongst other leadership and professional development activities, boost your visibility. Being more visible as a leader is about being seen as one with integrity. And being the first-person others think of when they need to call on the skills and knowledge you have. Being more visible keeps you front of the mind of the key decision makers and puts you at the head of the line for opportunities.

According to Mentorloop, an online mentoring access service, employees who receive mentoring are promoted five times more often than those who don't. Furthermore, 71% of Fortune 500 companies run mentoring programs[26]. In a *Harvard Business Review* article by Suzanne de Janasz and Maury Peiperl, 'CEO's Need Mentoring Too', they surveyed 45 CEOs who'd had formal mentoring arrangements. They said:

> *71% said they were certain that company performance had improved as a result. Strong majorities reported that they were making better decisions (69%) and more capably fulfilling stakeholder expectations (76%). More than anything else, these CEOs credited mentors with helping them avoid costly mistakes and become proficient in their roles faster (84%).*[27]

Mentors challenge, champion and educate. A great mentor will:

- help you read, deal with and even influence the culture and internal politics of the organisation.

---

26 'Human Reconnection: The New HR'. Mentorloop. Accessed at https://mentorloop.com/mentoring-program-benefits/.

27 de Janasz, Suzanne and Peiperl, Maury. (April 2015) 'CEOs Need Mentoring Too'. *Harvard Business Review*. Accessed at https://hbr.org/2015/04/ceos-need-mentors-too.

- teach you skills, especially if you are looking to shift from a technical individual contributor role to a people management role or a more strategic leadership role.
- be a strong, confident role model who can help you amplify your confidence and courage to step up.
- expose you to new ideas and perspectives.
- introduce you to new professional contacts, other senior decision makers and key industry players.

Mentoring for Visibility

Mentors can help you be more visible, depending on the type of mentoring, such as:

Role Model: They have skills or leadership you can observe and learn from to influence your own journey.

Sponsor or Broker: They have the connections and can call in favours or recommend or refer you for opportunities.

Advocate: They can be your cheerleader encouraging you to show up. They may accompany you to meetings and events you may not normally have access to.

There are many other famous mentoring matchups.

Oprah Winfrey once said of Barbara Walters, 'Had there not been you, there never would have been me'.

Bill Gates has referred to his long-time mentor, Warren Buffet, as 'one of a kind'.

As far back as 400 BC, Socrates mentored Plato. And Plato went on to mentor Aristotle, which goes to show that the student can become the master and the mentee can also be the mentor.

When you think about who could help you be more visible, who could be a mentor to you?

Find a Mentor

As a leader, who do you look up to in your organisation or industry? When it comes time to find a mentor you don't have to be limited by those who are right in front of you.

- Mentors can be internal or external to your organisation or industry.
- Mentors can be engaged for a short-term period or for the long term.
- Mentors can be younger or older than you.
- Mentoring can be formal or informal.
- Mentoring can also be virtual—as in you observe them from afar. They may never know they've been a mentor to you. Nelson Mandela is said to have been influenced by the books and writings of Mahatma Gandhi.

Start with knowing what you want from a mentoring relationship. What do you want your mentor to help you achieve? For example,

1. Help you increase your self-awareness and confidence.
2. Help you increase your leadership capability and preparedness for more senior opportunities.
3. Advocate for you or sponsor you for projects and opportunities.

When it comes time to identify potential candidate mentors, remember that you may not be able to engage your number one choice. So it's best to consider a few people who you admire.

List three to five potential mentors, don't think or try to judge if they would say yes to mentoring you, simply list who you'd like as a mentor.

_____

_____

_____

_____

Identify your goal

Before settling on a mentor, you must understand your own goal. Your mentor or mentors may or may not be working in the same organisation, or even industry so focus on potential mentors' skills, strengths, experiences and achievements that resonate with your goals and what you aspire to achieve. Finding someone that aligns with your goals is why it's important to look within your organisation, industry and beyond. Be mindful that a totally external view, a mentor from outside your industry, can provide some great challenges to perspectives.

What do you want from a mentor?

_____
_____
_____
_____
_____

Formalising Your Mentor-Mentee Relationship

To reach out and connect with your potential mentor, show genuine interest in who they are and what they are working on. Let them know why you admire them. Aim to build a relationship and to network with them. While networking you may be asking questions and it may feel like the mentoring has already begun. However, it's appropriate and respectful to formalise the relationship when you're seeking mentoring.

Formalising the mentor-mentee relationship will ensure you both use your valuable time effectively, are working towards your goals and have accountability to and with each other. This provides an environment where you have clear expectations of each other and the mentoring process. It's also critical to prepare and come to the mentoring arrangement willing to actively participate.

Key areas to cover to ensure a successful mentoring relationship:

1. Both mentor and mentee need to share their expectations of each other and the mentoring relationship.
2. Invest time in getting to know each other and your values and build a rapport.
3. Agree on your meeting agenda, timing, frequency and location.
4. Agree on topics that can be discussed and topics that are not open for discussion.
5. Determine how accountability will be handled and held.
6. Agree on an end date or review date for the mentoring relationship.

Demonstrating your gratitude for the mentoring time and advice will improve your own skills to speak up and communicate effectively. It will help you be a mentor to someone else one day. After all, mentoring is not a one-way relationship.

Length of Mentoring Relationship

Many mentoring relationships are for a defined amount of time while others are ongoing. Audrey Hepburn mentored Elizabeth Taylor throughout her career, and remained friends up until Hepburn passed away. While, like Audrey and Elizabeth, it's common for mentors and mentees to become firm friends, it's also okay when a mentee 'outgrows' the need for a mentor. The length of the relationship is firmly up to you and your mentor.

Consider becoming a mentor so you can become more visible and be seen

When done well, mentoring is fantastic for both the mentor and mentee. For me personally, mentoring has helped me achieve successes I never thought I ever would in my business. And mentoring has helped me achieve these successes faster than I would have if I had plodded and muddled along without the support and expertise of someone who has gone before me.

But the benefits aren't just for the mentee. Mentors can get a great deal of benefits from the relationship, including increased visibility.

As a leader, when thinking about succession planning or preparing your people to receive opportunities (say, through your delegating), you are likely already asking yourself who in your team could do with some mentoring. But are you also asking yourself who could *do* the mentoring? Are you asking yourself who you could mentor yourself?

Benefits of Being a Mentor

The benefits of being a mentor include:

- Improving your communication skills especially with holding people to account, challenging assumptions or limiting beliefs and giving feedback.
- Boosting your confidence as you see the confidence in your mentee grow.
- Learning more about yourself as you help your mentee reflect on the questions and insights you share with them.
- Expanding your networks.
- Being exposed to and learning from different perspectives.

A Note on Networking

When my husband and I returned to Australia from living in the United Arab Emirates we landed in Sydney. Neither of us knew Sydney or had lived in Sydney. Other than a few family members in Sydney, we knew no one and didn't have any network.

This return to Australia marked the beginning of my business so I had to get myself known in the market. I Googled networking and off I went. I set a goal of attending one networking event per week for six months. It was demanding but successful. I didn't just show up at networking events, I followed up and met with hundreds of people to learn about who they are, what they do, what they need, and how I could help them. By doing this, I was front of mind when clients were looking for the services I offered. I secured work because my network referred me.

By undertaking this networking, my confidence and influence in a new market increased quickly and significantly. The more networking I did, the more comfortable I was in asking for opportunities, the more others would reach out to me.

Igniting your visibility can be significantly positively impacted through networking. You don't have to attend one event every week like I did, however ask yourself who knows you?

With social media being so prevalent in our day to day lives, we can easily slip into feeling that a like, a follow or a connection is all that's required for networking. This is not networking. Engaging in conversations online and face to face, helping your network truly know you, equips them to be able to help you achieve what you want to achieve.

Janine Garner[28], one of Australia's leading networking experts, says you need a range of key people and personalities to help you be more visible:

1. People who can help you become more, they inspire you and cheer you on.
2. People who will help you be more through nurturing you and keeping you on track, steering you away from any negative emotions or concerns about your progress and what you want to achieve.
3. People who will teach you, they will help you know more so you have more wisdom to offer.
4. People who will help you do more as they will keep you accountable, push you to achieve more and mentor you.

Reflect on who you regularly network with, the people you see often when you attend internal meetings and functions and industry

---

[28] Garner, Janine, (2017) 'It's Who You Know: How a network of 12 key people can fast-track your success'. Wiley, Melbourne. (pp72-73).

events. Can you identify roles in any of them, for example, do any inspire you, nurture you, teach you, push you?

Practice: Networking for Visibility

Who helps you to become more: they inspire and cheer you on:

_____
_____
_____
_____

Who helps you be more: they nurture you; they keep you on track:

_____
_____
_____
_____

Who teaches you: they expand your knowledge and wisdom:

_____
_____
_____
_____

Who helps you do more: they keep you accountable, push you, mentor you:

_____
_____
_____
_____

What are the current internal (inside your organisation) networking opportunities?:

_____
_____
_____
_____

Are you a member of an industry association? What are the current industry networking opportunities?:

_____
_____
_____
_____

What are three local community networking events you'd be prepared to attend?:

_____
_____
_____
_____

Who are three key influencers in your organisation you are prepared to meet and network with?:

_____
_____
_____
_____

Networking Tips

1. Conversation Before Card

The days of thrusting business cards into the hands of strangers are gone. It feels so cold and off-putting to have someone walk up to you and force their business card onto you.

Bob Burg is a networking and referral expert and is famous for his quote, 'All things being equal, people do business with, and refer business to people they know, like and trust.' This applies no matter if you're trying to sell something, sell yourself to a senior leader, or sell a proposal to your team. People will find it difficult to consider you for opportunities, to see you as the leader they want to align with if they don't know you.

Build relationships by having conversations that connect.

2. Be Interested

Networking and building a network of people who can help you happens when you show interest in others. Ask questions, listen, be genuinely interested in learning about people. This helps you to learn how you can mutually help each other.

People, who feel as though you're interested in them, will usually be interested in knowing and helping you. This is natural reciprocity; people will generally want to help those who have helped them. This includes senior leaders you might meet at a company event; remember they are human too!

3. Follow Up

Connecting and networking at internal company or external industry events is the start of igniting your visibility through the strategy of being seen. Be sure to follow up with the people you meet, investing time to catch up with the people, one on one, demonstrates your interest and allows both of you to learn more.

Great people stand out from others by their visions and not much by their intelligence.
—Amit Ray

What did you wish you knew about self-leadership before you stepped into your first leadership role?

I wish I knew I didn't have to prove myself every single day.

Michelle Berriman
Executive Director, Fundraising Institute of New Zealand

Snap to watch the full interview.

Michelle's wisdom lies in learning pace and patience. Leaders want to do well and want to achieve the strategic objectives the organisation or business set. Pace and patience give leaders the space to be strategic, thoughtful, and the voice of calm, confidence and influence. Cutting yourself some slack, to not be perfect and prove yourself daily will give you the space to focus on being authentic, avoid burnout, and truly engage and feel empowered. It's not about giving up, it's about balance.

You can spark your self-leadership by learning to balance your own expectations while managing expectations of those around you.

CHAPTER FIFTEEN

STAND OUT: BACK YOURSELF TO GET OUT FRONT!

STRATEGY NINE

Peter was a stand out! In the entire five weeks of one of my university practicums (which is like an internship or work experience), I saw Peter do one thing and one thing only. He wandered the office floor with his football tipping folder in his clutches, stopping off at people's pods, offices and desks to update the tipping sheets.

As this practicum was based with a civil service, I'm 100 percent sure tax payers were not giving up their hard-earned tax payments for a full-time football tipping role. Employee experience is important but this was taking it too far. I asked another employee what Peter's role was, trying to give Peter the benefit of doubt that he did have a civil service function. The employee rolled their eyes and groaned, 'I think he has something to do with infrastructure but he mainly does the footy tipping'.

Clearly, Peter was a standout but not necessarily for the most positive of reasons. Unless you're a footy fan or an avid footy tipper!

Standing out will attract attention—but this could be positive or negative. The key is to act in a way that brings attention that adds to your success (rather than diminishes it).

How do you want to be seen by others?

Dylan, a regional manager, was a participant in one of my deep dive leadership programs. His main goal was to be promoted within the next 12 months. He knew what skills he needed to work on and he also knew that he needed to be more visible. He understood that to be a bit bolder and do things to stand out would fire up his self-leadership which, in turn, would positively impact his leadership and career advancement goals.

Until then, during management team meetings Dylan would hold back, listen and observe. He often felt as though he didn't have much to contribute, so he would sit towards the back of the meeting room and simply keep quiet. When meeting online he would leave his camera off, particularly when senior leaders were in attendance. It's not that he was shy. It was that he didn't want to be a show off or risk saying or doing anything that would reflect poorly on him.

Part of Dylan's leadership program action plan was learning more about the value of being more visible, including becoming more visible and getting feedback about his own visibility. He met with two peers, two senior leaders and two of his team to ask for feedback on how visible they believed Dylan was and what he could do to stand out for the right reasons.

The feedback was really encouraging. Everyone wanted to see and hear from Dylan more. His peers see him as clever and a good worker and he seems to handle issues really quickly and easily. One peer saw Dylan as a potential mentor but wasn't sure if Dylan would be open to it.

Dylan's direct reports saw him as a fair boss but were concerned that he didn't leverage his relationship with his peers, the management team, nearly enough. This meant that his direct reports would sometimes bear the brunt of the pressures from above, rather than Dylan seeking out support from and with his peers.

The senior leaders saw potential in Dylan and were pleased he was nominated for the leadership program. They hoped it would help him be more confident to speak up and therefore stand out, and share his ideas and insights amongst his peers. Dylan has solved some really complex team issues and the senior leaders felt that needed to be known across the management team—others could learn from him. Dylan however didn't see that as anything special to share.

One senior leader said, 'He needs to stop hiding his light as he'll miss out on opportunities. People will see it as him not being keen for advancement'.

Following the feedback sessions, Dylan immediately took some practical actions to stand out, including:

- Blocking off 10 minutes prior to meetings to ensure he was familiar with the agenda.
- Prior to meetings jotting down any ideas he had that might be shared during the meeting. Notes would help give him confidence to speak up.
- Always having his camera on for all online meetings.
- Arriving at face-to-face meetings early and sitting closer to the more senior leaders.
- Asking his direct boss if he could chair a meeting so he could get some practice being more visible amongst a more senior group and his peers.
- Putting himself and his top three direct reports through a presentation skills course so they could have more confidence, courage and influence during presentations and meetings.
- Scheduling time with one of the senior leaders to discuss how he could improve the effectiveness when he pitched ideas and proposals.

Dylan not only took action he shared this plan with his immediate boss and the senior leaders who he admired most. They were so impressed with how proactive he was they started competing to bring Dylan into their respective teams.

While Dylan's promotion didn't quite happen within the 12 months as per his goal, he was assured that as soon as a position became open it was his. He did win a company award within the 12 months and was promoted only a few months later.

Visualisation for the Win

Visualising is picturing in your mind what you want to achieve. It's imagining the outcomes you seek. While Dylan might not have thought he visualised his way to standing out, to some degree visualising his success helped him achieve success.

A study[29] compared people who worked to increase finger strength physically with people who simply exercised them virtually, that is, in their minds. The finding showed a 53 percent muscle strength increase in the physical exercisers. But it also showed a muscle strength increase of 35 percent in those who merely visualised the exercises. There's no doubt that visualising has a positive impact.

Practice: Visualisation

Visualise what you want to achieve. Being as specific as you possibly can, imagine using all your senses to picture the success you want. Ask yourself the following questions and write down your thoughts.

What do you want to achieve?

_____

_____

_____

_____

_____

---

[29] Ranganathan VK, Siemionow V, Liu JZ, Sahgal V, Yue GH. 'From mental power to muscle power—gaining strength by using the mind'. *Neuropsychologia*. 2004. Accessed at https://pubmed.ncbi.nlm.nih.gov/14998709/.

How does it look?

How does it sound?

What does it smell like?

What does it taste like?

What does it feel like?

What actions do you need to take to realise your visualisation?

_____

_____

_____

_____

What resources do you need to help you achieve it?

_____

_____

_____

_____

What obstacles might get in your way and who can help you remove those obstacles?

_____

_____

_____

_____

How does achieving it make you feel?

_____

_____

_____

_____

Vision Boards

Vision boards are effective ways to bring your visualisation alive and keep you motivated. A vision board is a physical representation of what you're visualising. It can be made up of a collection of words, images, icons, art and more that depict your goal. You can also create a virtual vision board using platforms such as Pinterest, Canva or Milanote.

Keep your vision board in a place where you can see it regularly so it can help keep you focused on your goal. It will help keep you motivated to achieve what you want to achieve. And this means the success you achieve will help you stand out for all the right reasons.

Checklist for Standing Out

From the below list, pick at least three you can start immediately to begin to stand out today.

- [ ] Always have your camera on and be present throughout all online meetings.
- [ ] Take your good manners to a whole new level—beyond 'please' and 'thank you'. Some ways you could elevate your manners could be, for example, to offer to help; remove bad language from your conversations; be sure to return things that you borrow; offer to help tidy up the communal space even if it's not your turn; remember and use people's names; hold doors open or offer to carry something when you see someone carrying things down the corridor. Small gestures make big impacts.
- [ ] Be reliable. Apologise if you have let someone down.
- [ ] When incidents or accidents occur, breathe and remain calm. Being poised doesn't excuse or ignore an issue but it helps you stand out and earn respect because you remain calm under fire, while focusing on problem solving.
- [ ] Posture. Be mindful of what your body language portrays. Would others observe you as confident?
- [ ] Go the extra mile.
- [ ] If you believe in your idea, take a breath, take a risk and share it.

- ☐ Adopt a mindset of being a lifelong learner. The more you learn the more it will help you to stand out as the go-to expert.
- ☐ Be yourself. Give yourself permission to show the best and genuine version of yourself.
- ☐ Have a good attitude. Your attitude will impact your resilience and give you energy to handle the more challenging aspects of your life.
- ☐ Dress for success. My grandmother always told me that if I wasn't sure how to dress for an event, dress up.
- ☐ Pay attention to the details. This shows you're professional and you care.
- ☐ Be grateful.
- ☐ Be kind to yourself and to others.
- ☐ Nominate yourself or your team for an award.
- ☐ Actively network. Expanding your network inside your organisation and across your professional life will help you stand out.
- ☐ Show interest. When you show interest in others you become interesting to others.

Practice: Standing Out

The three actions from the Standing Out Checklist that I will start immediately are:

1. _____
2. _____
3. _____

Knowing yourself is the beginning of all wisdom
—Aristotle

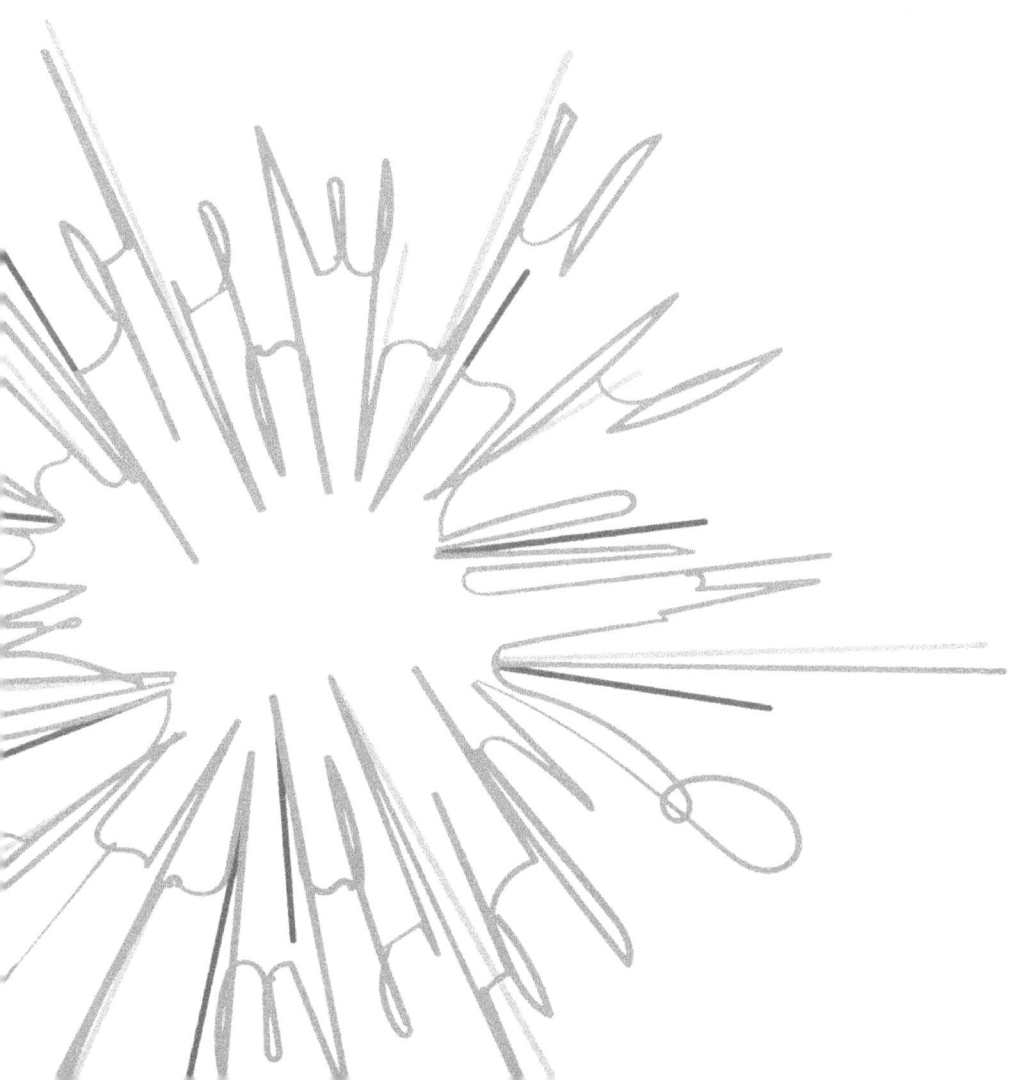

The Complete Spark Model

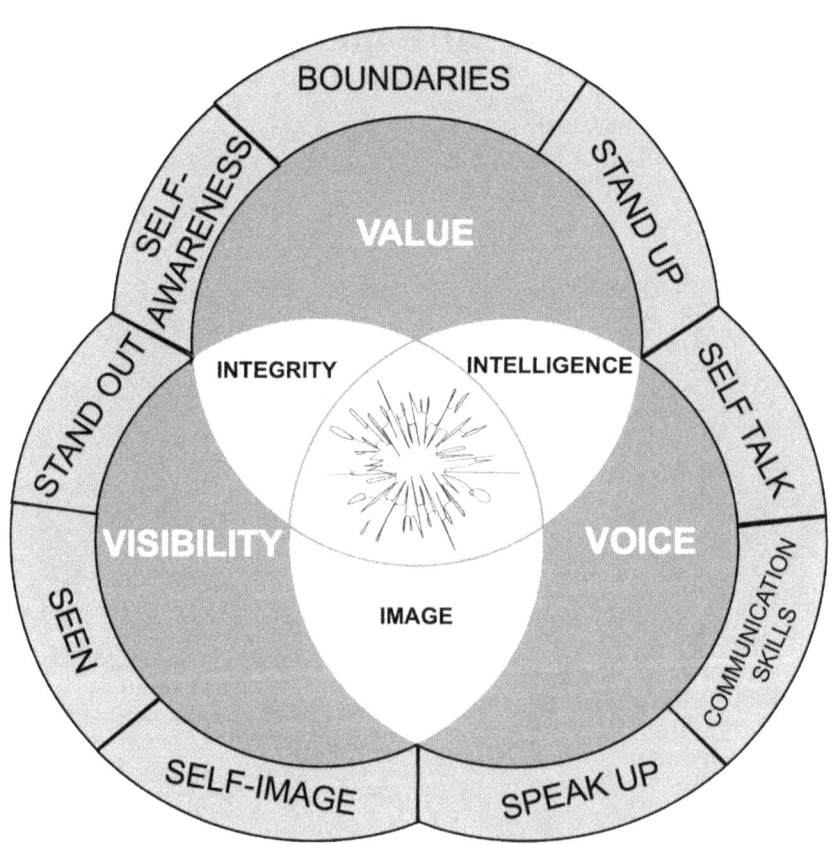

What did you wish you knew about self-leadership before you stepped into your first leadership role?

You're NOT expected to know everything!

Dominique Lamb
CEO, National Retail Association

Snap to watch the full interview.

> Leaders feel huge pressure to have all the answers, to be across every aspect of what's happening. This is unrealistic and impossible. Check in with yourself by asking if this is a real or perceived expectation. It's more than okay to not know everything. It's okay to invite others to be experts and collaborate.
>
> You can spark your self-leadership by reflecting on the expectations you have of yourself.

CHAPTER SIXTEEN

EXTRA SELF-LEADERSHIP SPARKING GOALS

Self-leadership can be sparked, built and sustained through a diverse range of goals. Here are 26 goals for you to work on implementing into your life and self-leadership.

Accountability

Self-leadership needs accountability. Great self-leaders will take accountability and responsibility for their feelings, thoughts and actions. This includes taking action to fix things when you miss a deadline or make a mistake and genuinely apologising where and when it's required without beating yourself up.

Build

Self-leaders build on their skills, knowledge and experiences and align them with their motivation and behaviours. Learning new things outside of a comfort zone expands knowledge, wisdom and perspective. This allows self-leaders to continuously build their confidence, courage and influence.

Compassion and Empathy

When you can understand the emotions and feelings of others and respond in such a way that another person can see you understand

and respect their feelings and views, this helps you both connect better.

Decision Making

Self-leaders are great decision makers. You need strong decision-making skills as part of setting goals and making plans that will determine your success. The first step to being an exceptional self-leader is deciding you want to be one.

Ego

A healthy ego is first, healthy self-respect, and second, a belief in yourself and your abilities. An overly strong ego (that is, being egotistical) can damage relationships, teams and leadership. It's not about removing ego—we all have an ego and it's needed for self-esteem—it's about making sure your ego is in check.

Feedback

Feedback helps you learn about yourself so that you can make adjustments and choices to better influence and lead yourself. Seeking and being open to feedback from a range of people will enable you to see even more strengths that you may not initially realise you have, and you will learn about other areas ready for development.

Goals

Goals can help motivate and with goal achievement your self-leadership enhances. The act of setting goals will help you improve, while the act of achieving goals will boost your confidence in addition to bringing you success.

Habit

You know that good habits result in greater successes. Greater successes then reinforce the value of positive habits. Develop the habit of actively enhancing your self-leadership so that you have the confidence, influence and courage to lead yourself and others effectively.

Interesting—Interested

It's nice to be thought of as interesting and to have others be interested in you. Being interesting comes from expanding your world view as well as your self-awareness.

One of the easiest and most effective ways to be seen as interesting is to be interested. So, be curious, be present, ask questions and show genuine interest in other people, places and points of view!

Journal

Journaling allows you to self-reflect, capture ideas, organise your thinking, set and achieve goals and inspire your creativity. Journaling is also a great way to express and regulate emotions as it allows you to get your emotions and feelings about a situation out on the page.

The journaling process can also help you get clear on your values, voice and visibility as it can boost your confidence to speak up clearly and confidently and stand out in situations that will lead to your success.

Kindness—To Self and To Others

Being kind to yourself means you give yourself less of a hard time when things go wrong and helps you to feel encouraged to try more things. Your self-kindness will show up in positive self-talk and positive self-image. Importantly, being kind and non-judgemental towards yourself equips you to be a kind, non-judgemental and compassionate leader.

Learning

Lifelong learning is knowing that there is always something new to understand. Acquiring new skills and knowledge helps you embrace challenges, stay relevant, remain healthier and ensures you feel more fulfilled.

Motivation

Motivation is what will drive your energy and focus to achieve, including pushing through challenges to meet and reach goals. Stay connected to your goals, build your network and engage a mentor to help boost your motivation through accountability.

Networking

Actively building a rapport with others and expanding your social and professional network will give you the confidence to speak up and stand out.

Optimistic

Being optimistic can help you see an issue as an opportunity. You can approach a short-term problem with the attitude of setting a plan to resolve or improve the situation. This is not about never being pessimistic or ignoring adversity but, in most day-to-day situations, is a method for looking positively for the way forward.

Personality

Learn about your personality, who you are, your style of behaving and your preferred method of communicating so you spark your self-awareness. Doing this enables you to be able to adjust and flex to all different people and situations.

Question

Self-leaders ask questions! Through questioning, and listening, they receive valuable information that helps them to create action plans and achieve the goals they set. Asking invites engagement, creativity and curiosity.

Regulate

Self-leaders will have great self-regulation. Emotional regulation is being able to identify and then control your emotions. Emotional intelligence is the ability to recognise, understand and manage emotions (intrapersonal communication) and the ability to recognise, empathise and relate to others (interpersonal communication). Both emotional regulation and emotional intelligence (as a vital part of emotional regulation) are core success factors of self-leadership.

Share your ideas

Your thoughts, insights and perspectives will enrich the lives of others. Even if they don't agree, you provide a perspective and food for thought. Many senior leaders share with me their frustration that their management team and their direct reports, don't speak up and share their ideas nearly enough. Most leaders desire input over perfection.

Trust Yourself

Focus on trusting yourself more. Believing in your own expertise, as well as your skills to problem solve, means you will have the courage to test and experiment without the fear that you'll be stalling progress.

Unconscious bias

Everyone has some form of unconscious beliefs about certain social groups. Expanding your self-awareness can help you to identify your unconscious beliefs or biases. Identifying them is the first step. The next is to work to understand and appreciate the differences and diversity that will give you an appreciation that can help improve your self-leadership and leadership of others.

> What did you wish you knew about self-leadership before you stepped into your first leadership role?

You're never always right!

Ask for help!

Jas Johal
Delivery Manager, Tech Industry

Snap to watch
the full interview.

Visualise

Visualising can help with a range of aspects that positively impact your self-leadership. If you visualise achieving your goals this can spark your confidence and boost your motivation. Consistently visualising success can help create new neural pathways in your brain that then help reinforce new positive habits.

Worthy

A leader with a low sense of self-worth will tend to be controlling, dictatorial and a micromanager. A leader with a strong and positive sense of self-worth will find it easier to empower, engage and encourage others through a range of activities, including delegating. Self-leaders think, feel and believe in themselves because acting to achieve goals takes self-worth.

What did you wish you knew about self-leadership before you stepped into your first leadership role?

You can't do it all. Put people in and delegate early.

Jeremy Fleming
Managing Director, Stagekings

Snap to watch
the full interview.

X-Factor

Learn your X-factor, your unique special strengths. When you know your strengths you can play to them, showcase them, use them to not just your advantage but also for the benefit of your colleagues, team and organisation. If you are unsure what your strengths are, ask.

Yardstick

Self-leaders set goals and work a plan to achieve them. A yardstick is a test, standard or model used for measuring, judging or comparing. What can be your positive and inspiring yardstick or measure to help you know when you've achieved a goal? How can this yardstick help you be more confident, influential and courageous?

Zig Zag

No one goes through this life unaffected by some form of adversity. Self-leadership is not about perfection. It's about knowing you can adapt, adjust and find your way through a situation. It's knowing that sometimes you will need to zig zag your way through, despite the desire for a straight line from A to B. The zig zag often gifts you a richer experience that boosts your resilience, wisdom and self-leadership. Embrace life's zig-zags.

FINAL WORD

Great leadership starts with exceptional self-leadership. The strategies in this book are designed to spark your self-leadership and inspire your success as a leader. Each strategy is designed to amplify your confidence, influence and courage to be a better self-leader, a better leader of others and a better you.

The skills and traits of successful leaders are numerous. Google it and you'll drown in lists upon lists that include things like communication, motivation, feedback, creativity, decision making, problem solving, productivity, strategic thinking, team building, managing change, and much more. To be able to be or do these things successfully leaders need self-confidence, the ability to engage and influence and the courage to act. The strategies in this book are designed to deliver these three elements for you by focusing on value, voice and visibility. But it's up to you to implement the strategies. Only you can do that for your own success.

Start small but start! Self-leadership is not about never having any problems or issues again. Life is full of trials and false starts. So, no matter if you stall, start again. You are worth it. Have you ever met a strong person who's had it easy all their life?

When you spark your value, voice and visibility you will have the confidence, influence and courage to stand up, speak up and stand out!

I would love to hear how you go implementing the strategies. Please reach out and share your stories and examples with me at sally@sallyfoleylewis.com.

Here's to your spark.

Sally

BOOK SALLY

Sally Foley-Lewis is a leadership and middle management expert. She speaks, mentors and runs workshops to help managers move and improve. She's helped many dedicated professionals become exceptionally productive and confident leaders.

Leaders who implement effective leadership development strategies, and build their self-leadership, will decrease employee turnover, boost engagement and increase profits, com pared to managers who are less effective at people management and leadership.

As a multi-award winning expert Sally positively impacts results, leadership and team performance. She's presented to, and worked with, 10,000+ managers and leaders from medium-sized to global companies across the world. She loves traveling the world – on planes and online – to help develop managers.

- 2021 USQ Outstanding Alumnus of the Year—Business and Enterprise
- 2021 A.I. Influential Businesswoman—Winner—Most Inspirational Leadership Development Specialist (Australia)
- 2020 Gold Stevie Award—Female Entrepreneur of the Year—Business Services
- 2020 Bronze Stevie Award—Female Entrepreneur of the Year—Consumer Services

- 2020 Breakthrough Speaker of the Year by Professional Speakers Australia
- 2019 finalist for Australian Learning Professional of the Year
- 2019 Australian Champion Sole Trader winner—Australian Small Business Champion Awards
- One of the 25 LinkedIn Top Voices for Australia for 2018 for her thought leadership.

PROFESSIONAL SPEAKER & FACILITATOR:

Keynote Speeches and Workshops (Live, Online and Face-to-Face)

- SPARK: Fire up your confidence, influence and courage through self-leadership
- One Day Leadership Retreat
- P.U.M.P: Pump Up My Productivity
- The Productive Leader
- The Big 3 Essential Skills Every Manager Must Master
- DELEGATE: Double the Results! Halve YOUR Effort!

See more: https://bit.ly/SFLspeak

If you're looking for a presentation, workshop or development program for your team please reach out. I'd be delighted to work with you to create a meaningful, energising and engaging experience.

Check out the **One Day Leadership Retreat** to ignite your management team's self-leadership: https://www.sallyfoleylewis.com/one-day-leadership-retreat/

This fully customised program is the perfect day to slow down to be more present, to energise and engage, while practically and dynamically applying the content of this book to ignite self-leadership.

E: sally@sallyfoleylewis.com
M: www.sallyfoleylewis.com
T: +61 3289 1409 or +61 401 442 464

Some of Sally's Clients Include:

Microsoft, QGAir, L'Oréal, Powerlink Qld, KSB (Kuwait), Cancer Council Qld, AIBB, AQNML, Tabreed, RBC Investor Services, Groupon, Canadian Shipping Line, Cognizant, Abu Dhabi Airport Company, Abu Dhabi Inflight Catering, ADNOC, Abu Dhabi Ship Building, Abu Dhabi Police, TAFE NSW, Qld Health, Sutherland Shire Council, Jump Carey, Mother Duck Childcare, CandK Assoc.

Praise for Sally's Work

You are a fantastic speaker on leadership. That you for sharing your wisdom and positivity.

—**Claire Stephenson**, Principal Hydrogeologist

I wanted to thank you so much for your session at the FIA conference on boundaries. I feel a bit better equipped to explain my boundaries, and examine my own boundaries, but also to help my team to identify their own boundaries. And for me, I feel like it's going to make a huge difference to my ability to understand in the workplace when someone might be reacting a certain way because a boundary has been triggered, and I think it's going to really help me in my career.

—**Brigitte Johnson**, Very Special Kids

Sally's 'Manage UP: Amplify Your Visibility, Voice and Value' presentation was engaging, high-energy, and showed a great sense of humour. She answered participants' questions with lots of 'how-to' that demonstrated her depth of experience and knowledge. Her visual diagrams clarified critical relationships and decision points so that people can quickly put ideas into practice. I truly enjoyed her presentation.

—**Richard Head**, President, Learning Wisdom LLC

Having interviewed Sally as a guest on my podcast, Journey Of The Successful Adviser, it was quite obvious she is not only a person of value and integrity, she is also extremely knowledgeable in her field of working with senior leaders to enable them to improve their personal performance – and impact the organisations they lead. It was a pleasure to learn more about Sally's journey and understand how she has built a reputation for her expertise.

—**James McCracken**, Mortgage Broker Consultant, The Successful Advisor

Sally sees the big picture and is able to pick and lead a team of trainers to achieve very positive outcomes for all. An over-achiever, Sally delivers excellent results and is very easy to work with. Her ethos is definitely grounded in service delivery and dedication to excellence.

—**David Fisher**, Owner/Director, Jedda Investment Group

Sally recently spoke at our Teachers Matter Conference in Brisbane. She was fantastic; knowledgeable, engaging and skilful. She led our teachers through understanding their personality types and that of others, to ensure they have the skills to work together productively in teams. Participants laughed, learned and had great aha moments. Thanks for being a joy to work with, entertaining, organised and fun!

—**Karen Tui Boyes**, CSP Spectrum Education

More testimonials: http://bit.ly/SFLwoohoo

Connect with Sally

LINKEDIN	www.linkedin.com/in/sallyfoleylewis/
TWITTER	twitter.com/SallyFoleyLewis
FACEBOOK	www.facebook.com/PeopleAndProductivity/
YOUTUBE	www.youtube.com/user/SallyFoleyLewis

SALLY'S OTHER BOOKS AND RESOURCES

The Productive Leader: Achieve More, Reduce Stress and Gain 2 Hours Per Day

https://www.sallyfoleylewis.com/books/the-productive-leader/

DELEGATE: Double the Results! Halve the Effort!

https://www.sallyfoleylewis.com/books/delegate-book/

Successful Feedback: How Leaders Can Increase Performance, Motive and Engage Their Team

https://www.sallyfoleylewis.com/books/successful-feedback/

Management Success Cards

https://www.sallyfoleylewis.com/books/management-success-cards/

Management Success Skills eBook

Grab your free copy here: https://www.sallyfoleylewis.com/contact/

The Professional Development Book Club

https://www.sallyfoleylewis.com/book-club/

Middle Managers Online Muster

https://www.subscribepage.com/mmom2022

www.ingramcontent.com/pod-product-compliance
Lightning Source LLC
Chambersburg PA
CBHW071912290426
44110CB00013B/1363